A NEW GOD
FOR AMERICA

BY

HERBERT PARRISH

THE CENTURY CO.

New York *London*

Copyright, 1928, by
THE CENTURY CO.

DEDICATION

This book is dedicated to the members of
the congregations of the Churches of St.
Mary the Virgin and the Advent in San
Francisco, St. Luke's Church in Baltimore
and Christ Church in New Brunswick,
among whom I served as rector for vary-
ing periods from 1898 until this present
year, 1928—and among whom I have
many friends.

PAX VOBISCUM

CONTENTS

PRELUDE TO A PERFECT DAY

It will be a perfect day when the members of churches, the theologues, the professors, the ministers, priests, bishops, the lay popes, the popes, and other eccleciastics and ecclesiastiarchs, male and female, cease their defensive polemics, their special pleadings, their apologies, their "Why-I-Am-What-I-Ams," their holier-than-thou attitudes, and turn upon themselves the microscope of criticism. There is some hope that this may sometime come about. Perhaps even this side of Paradise. Until now the churches and their members have been trying to tell the world just what advantages there were in being contributors to their own particular and special sects, in their own forms and ceremonies, in their peculiar beliefs and practices, in the singular type of pulpit manner their own ministers have, in the kinds of whiskers or no whiskers they permit them to wear, in the sort of hymns they sing, in the special cant they cultivate, in their unique record in the days that are past, in the glowing sancts and sanctesses who belonged to their sects some several hundreds of years ago. Each felt that it had a lead-pipe cinch on God. They got together, if at all, only against a common enemy, the paynim, the agnostic, the unbeliever, the atheist, the scoffer, the non-church-goer. Formerly they held out in joint forces against the theater, short skirts, Sunday movies, the saloon. But since Prohibition they have been increasingly divided on the subject of morals. In fact, they are at present more divided on morals than upon religious beliefs. The beliefs of Protestants are practically all the same. Their differences of doctrine are the differences between Tweedledum and Tweedledee. But up to the present time there is little sign that they will each begin the matter of criticism at home, look to themselves, correct themselves, find out the errors, defects, faults, failures, deficiencies, stu-

x

pidities, hokum, fraud, cant, and hypocrisy of their own systems.

So far such criticism has been confined to gatherings of the clergy behind closed doors. The clergy have to endure the brunt of the systems of which they are slaves and they know the situation. But even the clergy are not yet quite frank and honest about the matter. There is so much professional jealousy. The Rev. Mr. Whiterabbit would never let old Doctor Noodle know just what he thinks about things in general and his own parish in particular. Yet as the economic pressure squeezes them more and more, they do begin to loosen up and talk—confidentially, of course, and professionally, among themselves. One hears strange things nowadays at clerical gatherings.

But what a perfect day it would be if they should all cut loose and actually tell the raw truth, all of them, all at once. Tell what they really believe and think about the systems they are involved in without reservation and without fear. It would astonish the world. No more cant. No more hokum. No more sunny optimism. No more apologies and excuses. Just the raw truth. The actual facts. The seamy side. The inside of the cup.

Not that they would not have many beautiful things to say quite truthfully, things human and divine. They would. Life for the real man is full of such things—even in churches. But the systems, the inherited weight of theological and ecclesiastical traditions, the handicaps in spiritual work, in freedom, in truth, justice, beauty, and goodness. These are the things too seldom faced and elucidated. It is time somebody let such cats out of the bag. Here they go. Some of them.

Youth is the period of idealization. It is the time one falls in love. In love not only with the members of the other sex, but with theories, with systems. Conversion is such a falling in love. When a youth is converted he immediately idealizes the object of his affections, not only God, but the organization which has been the instrument of conversion, the society or church. It is the same if he chances to be converted to Marxian socialism, to atheism. He accepts everything about it, hook, bait and sinker. He becomes instinctively an apologist, a pleader. All excuses for defects recognized are valid. The ideal dazzles him. He questions but little. He accepts on authority. It is inevitable. There is no other way. It does not matter what he idealizes. So long as he idealizes it, that is enough. All human organizations flourish on the recruits from youth.

And as a lover of systems youth becomes austere, ascetic. There is no hardship that he will not endure. No self-immolation for which he is not ready. He will sacrifice everything, life itself, for the object of his affections. He is enthusiastic, delighted. It is all very beautiful. Very natural. Very real. So long as it lasts.

In the ministry, therefore, that is to say, in the Protestant ministry, youth is the most valuable of assets. The Roman Catholics keep them in obscure curacies until they have become disenchanted and mature. But in the Protestant churches young men receive generally much higher salaries than they will receive when they are old—unless they make a great success. The young minister has many "calls." The vestries, boards, trustees, deacons, or whatever they may be called, always hope great things from youth in the ministry. The ladies admire him. They

> Adore his doctrines and his hair
>
> And whisper, "What a good young man!"

During this period the young man, therefore, is naturally a stanch advocate of the system which has brought him out, supports, sustains him. It is all *couleur de rose* to him. It looks good.

The conviction that his church is the best possible church, the original, the perfect, the only true church in the world, may last a long time. Everything conspires to this end. It is the attitude known as loyalty. Just as in a college fraternity, a regiment, a club, every member of the same is expected to play the game, to boost, to crack up the organization to which he belongs, to be loyal. Like the natives of an Irish county to whom every outsider comes to be regarded as a foreigner of an inferior breed by the happy inhabitants, narrow, provincial, illiterate and ignorant themselves. It seems to be a merciful provision of Providence to satisfy the deficient with their lot. They regard all others with a just suspicion. Very great rogues in the system always encourage this provincial attitude. It makes things easier for the leaders. The leaders are always talking about the "blessings of loyalty."

But God is not merely the Hound of Heaven gifted with a keen scent for souls and with a limited enclosure into which He herds the gathered sheep. God is also the Ultimate Truth. When America was discovered men began to ask whether it was possible that God had left the inhabitants of so large a portion of the globe in a condition of darkness and total depravity all the years since creation while He showered upon western Europe the sole rays of His Truth. It was upsetting. Conceivably there were other and different ways in which the divine light had been shed abroad. Perhaps the other ways were just as good, perhaps they were even better. Particularly as things did not seem somehow to be entirely and permanently satisfactory in the accepted system. So they began to look abroad with a new curiosity and a sympathetic interest. Only the great rogues sought to repress them.

Something of the same sort happens to the youth emerging from his enamored provincialism into a wider experience. Just as an Irishman coming from the county Cork may find that the inhabitants of America are at least human. Only it happens in America that every effort is made to keep up the old home religious environment and racial traditions so that we have little pools of racial ingrown groups instead of a general national melting-pot. The Greeks, the Italians, the Hungarians, the Germans, the Irish and the rest can be quite as provincial and foreign here as they were at home. It is this spirit of narrow outlook and experience that the religious leaders so often encourage under the name of loyalty. It is loyalty to their little and generally obsolete systems, but it is not necessarily loyalty to Truth. And its basic necessity is economic. The leaders need the money.

It is the same with American sectarianism. This always follows the narrow lines of race tradition. The sects are essentially racial. And if the Roman Catholic Church seems to cover these by a general blanket of title, it is merely fiction, not a fact of unity. The racial lines are quite as truly drawn inside that body as they are out of it. There are German Catholic churches, Italian, French, Irish, as parochial in their outlook as any other under Protestant names.

Now the trouble with all this narrow, crude provincialism, as I see it, is that it arises and is kept alive by blind leaders of the blind who often through their own interest and probably more often through their own ignorance teach that the means of religion are the end of religion. There are a great many people in churches who imagine that formal conformity to the outward standard of the church insures them in the attainment of the object of religion, eternal life in God. This was the mistake that the Jews made at the time of Christ and it is the mistake that innumerable Christians have been making ever since. If you adhere faithfully to the system you will arrive surely in heaven. There is no truth in it.

Only the immature in mind and experience can endorse such a theory. The older one gets the more one becomes convinced that it is quite possible to be zealous in a cause that has no validity. Enthusiasm is not the test of reality. Loyalty should not be directed towards a system, but towards truth. It is the highest loyalty sometimes to shatter the system that truth may prevail. They are great rogues who stir up a false loyalty to false systems for their own advantage.

It will be a great day of judgment, therefore, when the members of churches cease to clamor about their own superiority and begin to ask themselves what is the matter with the systems to which they adhere. And this applies also to the whole of Christianity, to all the churches combined in relation to the other religions in the world.

Heretofore religion has been a matter of group or mass psychology. But emancipation from the tyranny of numbers is something to be accomplished by the individual. Young and ignorant people are swayed by the crowd. The critically intellectual man emerges. He emancipates himself from the opinion of the group. He sees beyond it. Every advance in history has come from such an attitude of independence. Science and art, statesmanship and discovery, depend upon the individual for every gain through the ages. The Creative Principle of the universe moves, like the sunrise, by lighting the peaks first.

And in religion especially it is the individual that counts. No matter what conclusions one arrives at in religion, these must be attained by individual effort. Children and the ignorant may be satisfied by repeating by rote formulas presented to them by authority. But when a man begins to think, he must think for himself if he is to make thought his own. He must justify in the forum of his own conscience the conclusions which he accepts. He must think things through before they have any real meaning for him.

A religion that penalizes thought, that fears free inquiry and frank discussion, must be a very weak religion. Its leaders are probably great rogues who, ignorant themselves, design to keep others ignorant and lashed to a false standard of loyalty to themselves rather than to Truth in order that they may retain their positions of trust and emolument. That there are such men cannot be doubted. In churches a man's chances of "preferment," of favor with the authorities, depend, not upon his sincerity and fearless stand for Truth as he sees it, but solely upon the amount of money he can give or get others to give for the support of the enterprises of the institution to which he belongs. He must show deference to his superiors and sing small in their presence, if he is to win favor. To prize up the lid and to show the folly and defects of the system is to be blacklisted at once. The system, therefore, in which authority is most securely entrenched, arbitrary and monarchical is always most potent among the ignorant. Men of intelligence, independence, self-determination and individuality cannot abide it. Education is its enemy. Thought is its bane. Knowledge is its destruction.

Nevertheless, the fundamental elements in almost any system of religion, certainly of the Christian religion, are of enormous value both to society in general and to the individual in particular. The system may be so bad that it thwarts and hinders it in some measure, but the idea of God in relation to the world shines through. Where men have lost all recognition of the divine in life, things grow pretty bad rapidly. To live solely for time and sense, for the objects of material life, is to become a brute. The ideal of Justice, Mercy, and Truth is essential for the salvation of the world. Religion is the most important thing in life. The systems should be devised to set it forth rather than to obscure it.

But it is not sufficient merely to set forth the ideals of religion. At least to be apprehended by the individual they must be thought through. The trouble with the churches is that they have loaded themselves up with mechanisms, obsolete theories, bankrupt customs, diverting the mind from the consideration of the really essential and simple elements of religion. A man can get on better with less than they offer rather than with more, less, that is, in quantity and more in quality. A deeper faith in God and a more sincere love of one's neighbor would be better than an expert knowledge of theology and ritual. For this reason one often finds men who are better Christians outside of the churches than some of those who are formal members.

For my own part I am rather a conventionally orthodox, strict churchman. I like the niceties of theology and the formalities of ritual. I am a Catholic, in the Western sense of the word, in religious taste. I prefer elaborate, ornate, gorgeous ceremonials. Splendid architecture for churches. Plenty of lights. Colored vestments. Incense. Processions. Solemn masses. Ethereal music. The historical background, the dignity, and the symbolism appeal to me. I can put up with a good deal of sheer superstition. It does not offend me at all.

These pages are not written to upset the religion of other people. They are written to make them, if possible, think through their positions. To justify them in their own minds. I am not wedded to the theories here advanced. Some may be sound and some may not be sound. So long as the reader reaches for himself a valid conclusion, satisfactory to himself, that is all I seek. The probabilities are that in any case he will come in the course of time to change them. Ultimate Truth is not reached by anybody all at once. Perhaps it will be a long time before anybody does really reach it. The theologues think that they have it now. But I have noticed even in the last few years that most of them who do any thinking at all have changed their opinions about a good many matters that I had thought in my salad days had been forever settled centuries ago. When we are young we are sure. But Truth has a way of expanding its borders.

America is now the greatest country in the world—in wealth, in commerce, in invention, perhaps in scientific knowledge. In education as an opportunity for all it is unsurpassed. We have more free educational institutions to the square inch than any other nation on the green globe. But we are still young in artistic and spiritual attainment compared with Europe. Our cultural standards are low. We have a good deal to learn. We have made some little beginning in music. In the other arts we are still in the iron age. And in religion we have nothing to offer except an emotional and indiscriminating generosity for every humanitarian cause that comes along. In religious expression we are barbarians in the stone age. At best we merely imitate the worst aspects of the traditional race inheritances of Europe. We have developed nothing original, nothing national, nothing peculiarly American. A majority of the best among us keep aloof from the activities of churches, from religious expression altogether. They are disgusted with the absurd crudities in worship, the dull drab stupid services, the emotional revivalism, the lack of color, beauty, dignity, and power. Roman Catholicism has the best chance of survival, if one counts compact organization, homogeneity, absolute authority, and a dominant sacerdotal caste. The Methodists with their strong system come next. And the Baptists, enamored of their peculiar type of individualism, follow. But Rome's domination by a foreign monarch, the Pope, makes it still a foreign religion. And like the others Rome does not stand the test of intellectual inquiry. The American religion of the future must be a religion that will at once engage the enthusiasm of the masses and at the same time justify itself to the enlightened and critical intelligence of our people. It must have simplicity and dignity. It must include beauty. It must be real. It must demonstrate actual power.

These little speculative essays and sketches, then, are an effort to show some of the inadequacies of our present religious condition in this country and to move the national consciousness in the direction of some determined undertaking for the elimination of them. The rubbish must be recognized and cleared away before constructive work can begin. *Religio Americana* will doubtless strike out new lines for the future.

The lack of unity and some repetition, of both thought and phraseology, which the patient reader will discover are due to the fact that most of the essays and two of the sketches were published at intervals during the past two years in magazines. Thanks must be given to the "American Mercury," "Atlantic Monthly," "Century," "Harper's," and "Religion" for permission to reproduce them here.

A NEW GOD FOR AMERICA

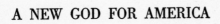

A NEW GOD FOR AMERICA

I

WHAT this country needs—much more than a good five cent cigar—is a new God.[1]

Let me explain. By *new* I do not mean a God newly created. I mean a God newly apprehended. In the language of philosophy, *new* is here used subjectively, not objectively. In short, I mean a new *conception* of God.

A God, to be worth anything, must be very old. Very old, indeed. He must, in fact, be eternal. In the words of the Catholic Catechism, God always was, is, and ever shall be. There is a nice problem, that mystics love, about the relation of time to God. They conceive that there is no time for Him at all—that He simply is,

[1] Former Vice-President Marshall said, "What this country needs is a good five-cent cigar."

3

and that our past, present, and future are limitations that do not apply to Him. He is, in that sense, always new, new every morning. But we generally think of God as very old. Before the earth and the world were made, before the morning stars sang together, God was. Men have gone crazy trying to conceive how old He is. The guesses of philosophers and the dreams of poets fail here. Centuries before Christ the Hindus speculated about His age. They conceived of Brahm breathing out universes and breathing them in again. They held that this was His fifth long breath and that He had already begun to draw it in. There will be at least two more.

Be that as it may, the idea of a new God for America is imperative. Any one can see that the old Gods of this country are entirely inadequate. They neither meet the needs of the time nor comport with the dignity of the nation. They are out of date, like the divinities in a Wagner music drama. The age has passed beyond them. Moreover, there are too many of them. Their number

4

has become confusing. A great nation should have only one God—a God sufficiently great to swallow up all lesser deities. We need a truly national God. He should be of a sort that compels the respect, nay, the reverence, the adoration, the enthusiasm of the people. Learned and ignorant should bow down before Him. To fail to worship Him should spell death. He should be able to scatter the inadequate "gods many and lords many" that now divide the nation and bring it into contempt. He should absorb all inferior deities into His own splendid and universal Personality.

The idea of a new God in this sense entirely comports with the teaching of the schools. The theologues themselves can find no fault with it. The learned doctors of divinity are already committed to it. Catholics and Protestants, heretics and orthodox, rectors and curates, priests and preachers, bishops and archbishops, popes and prelates, ritualists and revivalists, all the ecclesiastical brotherhood, endorse the idea. They strive for nothing else. It is what they want, what they are endeavoring to put across. Even the Holy Book itself, the Bible, is full of the conception of a new God, a God Who is a development, a growth.

II

COME with me for a little lesson. Take down from the shelf the old family Bible. Dust its venerable shiny covers. Open its pages: your grandfather read them. Learn that in the time of the Judges the God of the Jews was a fierce tribal Being named Yaveh. He was little better than a pirate, a yeggman, a peterman, a stick-up man. More ruthless than the modern bandit or robber, He murdered helpless women and children. His mouth was smeared with the blood of His victims. He spoke in the thunder and rode upon the wings of the wind. His nostrils breathed in the smell of burnt sacrifices and the smoke of flaming thuribles: He stirred up His votaries to make war upon their enemies. Whole cities were

6

destroyed by His command. The Jews called Him jealous.

Later on, you will see that as the conquered country of the Jews became settled and civilized and began to put forth abundant harvests, the gentler Baal *motif* came in. A new God began to be worshiped. The old name, indeed, remained, but Yaveh was no longer the crude savage, the ogre of the earlier period. He became softened, more reasonable, more convivial. He was the God of commerce, of the harvest, of social life. The smiling fields, the rich foods, trade, prosperity, plenty, revealed a new God. The priests began to moderate the severity of their ritual. Soon there was danger that the new God would become a degenerate God. Pleasure, rioting, revels, drunkenness, sex, began to appear in the religion of the people. Always, in time of prosperity, a danger. It became necessary for the Prophets, stern ascetics from the mountains, lean preachers of righteousness, to insist upon a limitation of the Baal concept.

God must include morality if the nation was to live. So the Law was devised. The Ten Commandments, attributed by the pious to a revelation given to Moses by God Himself on Mount Sinai, but actually worked out by Jewish statesmen from other national codes, fixed the morality of the Jewish God and of the Jewish people. It was a limited morality, to be sure, but it has been recognized ever since as a most effective device for national preservation. It kept the Hebrew people alive amid the softening and deteriorating influences of the Oriental tribes by which they were surrounded. It stamped the race with an enduring quality that remains even to this day.

For the Law was the enunciation of principles without which it is impossible for a national life to be secure. It was a wonderful discovery. The Commandments are in the sphere of sociology what gravitation is in the sphere of physics. And the discovery that God was a God of Law made a new God for the Jewish people. The Command-

8

ments were the discovery of a natural law, an invention like the lever of Archimedes. But since the Being who made nature and its laws included them in His works, it became necessary to conceive of Him in a new way. This discovery was as important to history as the humanism of the Greeks or the jurisprudence of the Romans. Perhaps more important.

Some centuries later, in the time of the second Isaiah, the God of the Jews changed still further. He had been up to this time a God confined to a nation, to the land. His interest was only for one little country and one little tribe. Now His sovereignty was extended to the nations of the world—though He was still very partial to people with a certain kind of nose. "The isles shall wait on Him." The book of Jonah is a little Jewish novelette written as propaganda for this idea. It was good for business. In short, every three or four centuries, from 1000 B.C. to the Christian era, the Jews got a new God. And why not? The whole world was progressing out of a state of savagery and barbarism into a higher and higher civilization. The God of the savage is one thing; the God of the civilized man quite another. What the one dotes upon the other simply cannot imagine.

This progress among the Jews was recorded in a series of little books which, when bound together and reëdited, we call the Old Testament. It is a superb record of human thought and experience, embroidered with poetry and legends, containing folk-lore and old traditions, worth little as history taken literally, but when studied intelligently, of supreme interest. No other nation of antiquity produced anything so good.

There was really nothing new in the God of Jesus. He took the best of the Jewish ideas about God and added a touch of genius. God became the Eternal Father, the Universal Spirit. "God is love." The savage Yaveh was thus lost in the mists of the past, and the Christian God arose to claim the allegiance of mankind.

10

It remained for the theologians, Greek and Latin, to attempt to clarify the Gospel conception. They defined the Trinity, the three Persons in the Godhead. This dogma they still insist upon.

III

Some years ago two women, immigrants from Europe, were overheard conversing in the steerage as their ship approached New York.

"What church you goin' to when you get to America?" asked one.

"Church!" exclaimed the other. "Why, there been't no God in America!"

The woman was wrong. There are a great many Gods in America. In fact, an actual count shows over two hundred of them. Probably there are a great many more. That is exactly our trouble. Here is a great nation, just entering upon its career as the chief power in the world, stupendously rich, highly inventive, emotional, religious, imaginative, clever, which has no grand outstanding God, universally recognized and respected, but only a surplus of mediocre, middle-class divinities, many of them as absurd as the idols in a Chinese pagoda.

"In God we trust," says the legend on our coins. But the trouble is to know *which* God. It is true that all the different Gods are called by the same name. They are all "God." But in reality they vary greatly. We have, for instance, the Billy-Sunday-William-Jennings-Bryan God. This God, modeled upon the most ancient and worst aspect of the Jewish Yaveh, is the God of Prohibition. His main characteristic is apparently to make people uncomfortable. He delights in little negative restrictions and petty taboos. His priests are not allowed to smoke or play cards. It is sacrilege for His votaries to drink a glass of beer. Wine stinks in His nostrils. Gin draws the lightning of His wrath. A vast following of fanatical devotees of the Upshavian type pray daily to this strange antique God. His adherents advocate force as the corrective of

12

character. They consider the laws of our legislative bodies to be of divine authority. Compulsion is as congenial to them as it was to the Moslem hordes who followed Allah. If they have not yet taken up the sword, they have been known to wield an ax. A queer, violent, uncomfortable, nagging, legalistic sort of God Who does not believe in evolution.

We have also certain medieval Gods, Gods Who inhabit great churches where they are approached through elaborate and spectacular forms and ceremonies, Gods Who can only be reached, apparently, through the intercession of saints, like St. Louis of Gonzaga and the Little Flower. And then there are sickly, sentimental Gods living in dingy buildings where they are worshiped by elderly vestals arrayed in rusty black gowns which come to their ankles—vestals who sing through their noses and whose chief mark of piety is their lack of style. Also, there are fashionable Gods, confined to and approached only in the most exclusive and select

13

of ecclesiastical edifices, small and Gothic, where it is considered a desecration if you speak to a stranger who happens to come in. In the vestibules of the temples of these Gods you often see an inscription which reads, "The Lord is in His Holy Temple." They take care that He never gets out.

The adherents of these various Gods, in the degree that they are devoted, hate each other with unrelenting antipathy. They divide the people. They inhibit any unity of spirit or action in the nation. Their differences are more separative than rank, color or race. What this country needs is one supreme God that shall unite its religious emotion and centralize its loyalty.

An obvious objection must be met here. It may be asked whether, since all these various Gods have the same name, They are not in reality one God, with only superficial differences. But it must be evident that the same question might be raised about the supreme Deities of all the pagan cults. Are not Brahm, Wotan, Jupi-

14

ter, and Zeus the same? They were all called God. Names, in fact, do not matter. What matters is the differences in attributes, in qualities. The various Gods in the American Pantheon are really quite different. It is for this reason that Their adherents express their devotion in such different ways. Their Gods produce quite different effects upon them.

Undoubtedly, there are certain common characteristics in the mass of American Gods. They all claim to be Biblical. And certainly They are all conspicuously anthropomorphic. They are Biblical because Scripture is used to enable Their missionaries to describe Them. And They are anthropomorphic because few people can escape the necessity of making God in their own image. Also, it is clear that most of these Gods rule a geocentric world and inhabit what Dean Inge calls a geographic heaven. Their earth was made in six literal days. Above it, in some remote place which nobody has ever seen, They sit enthroned in glory. They have long white

15

whiskers and, when people pray, They incline Their ears. They are very old men. Very far off. They never have any actual relation to life on this earth. On Sundays people talk to Them, or rather at Them, in churches, but during the week They are carefully locked up. It might be awkward if one of Them got out and turned up at the store. That *would* cause a row. And of course, while people pray to Them, they do not really expect that They will do anything about it. It is just one of those old customs.

Thus, at the present time a veritable *Götter-dämmerung* is taking place in America. The old out-worn, obsolete Gods are dying. Multitudes who formerly worshiped Them no longer believe in Them. Their churches in many instances are almost deserted. They cannot pay Their debts. Their priests and ministers starve. Nobody heeds their howling. Efforts are made from time to time to revive Them, but the revivals fail.

So the time is at hand for the creation of a

16

new God for America. We should indubitably have One. But His creation will be no light task. Even genius of the highest order is scarcely sufficient for it. It will take, no doubt, a generation or two to build up an adequate God for this great people. The new Gods of history did not spring suddenly into being. It took years of labor and strife to devise and promulgate One.

IV

This new God for America must appeal to the imagination. A God, to be a God at all, must be believed in. You cannot believe in something that you cannot imagine. It used to be maintained that belief was a matter of will, but there is really no such thing as a will to believe. A lot of perfectly good people have been executed because they could not adjust their imaginations to the beliefs that the authorities of their age required of them. We are just coming to understand that imagination, rather than will, is the

17

important factor in life, and, if in life, then in religion.

It is just because people can no longer visualize the Gods of the past in their imaginations that the old Gods are dying. The modern world pictures the universe, not as a thing moving around this earth, but as an infinite spread of stars, with the solar system occupying only a remote and obscure corner—with the earth a midge, a speck, a little ball of mud and fire spinning through the spaces around the sun. Heaven is not above, for there is no above. What is over our heads now will be under our feet at midnight. God cannot sit in heaven, for there is nothing to sit on. The preposterous anthropomorphism of the Bible does not fit the facts of the world. The imagination is unequal to the task of visualizing the eternal Creative Energy, omnipotent, omniscient, that has brought the worlds into being. We can postulate that He must have certain qualities, however. He must have power. He must have beauty. He ought to have goodness. Certainly He is truth. The imagination may be incapable of visualizing such a Being but it can work in that direction. It is at least not compelled to form a picture that it knows to be false.

The old Biblical conception of God did well enough for people who thought that the earth was a flat disc, that it was made in six days, that the sky was the floor of heaven. But the man who has some knowledge of geology and astronomy cannot accept the ideas of crude Hebrew barbarians of two thousand years ago. The Jews themselves found out what they did find out by their observation of the world about them as they knew it. The modern American will not confine his conception of God to the pictures of Him drawn in an age of defective knowledge. He will derive his Deity, not from any single book but from all books—not only from books written by the hands of men, but from the book of Nature as well. Here the pages are the rocks of the everlasting hills, the punctuation marks

19

are the stars, the illuminations are the sunrise
and the sunset, the printed word is stamped on
every field and flower. Thus the new God will
be vaster than the old one in relation to time
and space. His omnipotent sweep will be wider,
His glory more resplendent.

The new American God will not be confined
to buildings and to one day in the week. Religion, at bottom, is a philosophy of life. It
deals with the whence and why of things. A God
Whose laws run all through the universe is not
to be crowded out of the affairs of daily life.
He must be reckoned with. If He is the God of
Nature and of Nature's laws, then it is preposterous to think of Him only an hour on Sunday, or of worship as being anything less than
the whole of life. The scientist, the man who
builds a bridge, is quite as much a worshiper,
so long as he follows the laws of his science, as
the singer of psalms. The artist who paints in
accordance with truth and beauty is a servant
of the Living God quite as truly as the preacher

20

in his pulpit. The philosopher and the statesman who proclaim His truth are quite as religious, even technically, as the prophet who of old declared, "Thus spake the Lord."

Thus it is evident that the new American God will not be derived exclusively from the Bible. The old American Gods have always been taken right out of its pages, at least the Protestant Gods. The Catholic God is philosophical, theological, ecclesiastical rather than Biblical. The Catholic God is defined by Authority. But the Protestant God is purely Biblical. It is curious what a strange idea many Protestants have about the Bible. With them it comes first. First the Bible; then God. No God without the Bible. With such Protestants it is the Book that makes God, not God Who made the Book. Or rather, God *did* make the Book. He wrote it in the King James version and let it down out of Heaven by a string, that people should know something about Him and His doings. A wonderful revelation! Nobody could possibly know anything

about God if it were not for the Bible. That is
the way in which some Protestants regard the
Bible and God. With them God is in the Book.
He seldom gets out of it. Hence, He is necessarily a Fundamentalist.

But the new American God will not be confined to the pages of a book, not even those of
the Bible. He will rather be the God of the Universe, the Maker of all things, the First Cause,
the Creative Energy, the Source of power,
beauty, life, intelligence, personality. He will be
the God of truth, of reality, of facts. He will
make Himself known not through authority, but
through experience. For above everything else
this new God will be the God of law. Not of
human law but of divine law. That is to say, He
will be the God of things as they are. He will
not be a person. He will, however, have personality. A person is an individual and therefore
separable. But personality must be contained in
the Deity, since personality is a feature of the

Universe—is found in the Universe, in ourselves.

Whatever is found in the effect must be originally in the cause. And here we come to the difficult problem of Evil. People are always declaring that there cannot be a God since there is Evil—since their houses burn up, since they can't pay the mortgage, since they have the toothache, since the *Lusitania* sank, since there is such a thing as war. But this is to assume that we know all the purposes and ends of the universe from the slight observation we are able to make here and now. I'm not so sure about that. For one thing, we never would get anywhere if it were not for Evil. It has been the whip of civilization. We do what we do because of it.

> Then, welcome each rebuff
> That turns earth's smoothness rough,
> Each sting that bids nor sit nor stand but go!

But the problem of Evil makes a nice little

23

essay by itself. You can regard it as negation, as a limitation of good, as a condition of growth, as a disciplinary condition for improvement. But you cannot altogether be content with the Christian Science idea that it is an illusion. Not if you have the hives.

However let us leave something to be worked out. A God Who lacked mystery would scarcely be worth His salt. And the new American God must have not only the vague shadows of the remote past of His being to shroud Him, and the splendors of creation to veil Him, but ultimate purposes and an infinite variety of methods that we cannot expect to measure. If we get a glimpse of His glory, that is enough.

V

We must insist that our new God shall be a unity. To a large number of unequivocally trained minds the Christian dogma of the Trinity has brought only confusion. It is not too

24

much to say that a good many Christians are tritheists, or at least worship two Gods. But the most important truth that modern science has brought out is the unity of the universe and its laws. Things are the same here and in Calcutta. The same rules hold for the sun and for Sirius. There is one operative power throughout the great whole. Therefore, the new God must be one. The Trinity confuses people. I do not say that there is not a Trinity; what I say is that a good many people have erroneous ideas about it and that they lose something valuable in failing to realize the unity of God.[1]

[1] If the Protestant churches would use the Athanasian Creed to correct the misapprehensions that are derived from the constant use of the Apostles' and Nicene Creeds, they would avoid this difficulty. The Athanasian Creed was the final fruit of the religious controversies on the Trinity and the Incarnation in the Early Church. It makes clear the fact that there is but one God and it also distinguishes between the human and the divine natures in Jesus, as the other creeds do not. But the churches are afraid of offending people with the "damnatory clauses." Modern Protestantism lacks the courage of its convictions. This Creed is used in the Roman Catholic

But above all the new American God will be a God of law, of ascertained scientific law. Just as the ancient Jews, finding out certain truths that were of value in establishing their nation, made them articles of religion, so the modern world, finding out certain truths of the Universe and of life, will include them in the list of things ordained by its new Deity. As the prophets of old proclaimed, "Thus saith the Lord," so now the tested experience of our men of science will say with equal or more certain validity, "This is the law; this is God's law." The creative process, therefore, will not be presented to us under the old literally interpreted guise of a creation in six days. It will be a matter of geologic ages, of vast reams of time, of growth, of evolution. Most intelligent people have already accepted this idea. Man will not be conceived of as having been made from the

Church and in the Church of England. It has made impossible in those churches the kind of controversies that rage among American Protestants.

26

dust of the earth, and woman from Adam's rib. Man will be the ultimate product of that marvelous creative energy which can endow a minute speck of protoplasm with such emotional instinctive wisdom that it can develop into human form and human brain. The Fall of Man will not be considered as an act of disobedience to an arbitrary command not to eat apples in a garden with a woman. It will be thought of as a gradual rise of human life out of lower forms, through savagery and barbarism into civilized society. Sin will not be condemned as the deliberate choice of wicked courses on the part of the bad. It will be studied under the forms of race inheritance. The mercy and forgiveness of the new American God will not be the arbitrary acts of a capricious Deity. They will be the deliberate operations of inevitable laws working in relation to the human will. We shall not be saved from a hot hell, alive with worms and roaring with flames. We shall emerge rather into a consciousness of our heritage in the

Great Whole, which is the Kingdom of God.

It is worth consideration whether this idea, after all, was not very much what Jesus taught about God. The work of Jesus has been enormously perverted. He has been presented to mankind as a sort of spectacle, a dramatic protagonist, Who came out of the Beyond to perform on this earth a miracle-play by the contemplation of which men would be saved. The churches have stressed the teaching *about* Him, the teaching of St. Paul and the Creeds and the theologians. They have overlooked almost entirely the teaching *of* Him. The teaching *of* Jesus is far more important than the teaching *about* Jesus. The teaching *of* Jesus presents, under the term Kingdom of God, certain possibilities for human consciousness that are entirely suitable for an apprehension of the new American God. He had a consciousness of His relation to the Creative Energy of the Universe, which He called the Father, combined with a perception of certain psychological and sociological laws,

28

which He regarded as important for people to grasp. They constitute a veritable rule of divine procedure, the Kingdom which was His Good News. It was too good for the Jews and it is too good for many Christians. This conscious *rapport* with the Divine made Him the Son of God. The Jews regarded His claim, not understanding it, as blasphemy. They crucified Him. But His value to us at the present time is exactly this. His human soul had attained the fifth octave in the scale of existence. It was joined to and illuminated by the Eternal Word.

Something of the same sort of thing takes place in the mind of every man who thinks. And it gives a hint in regard to the possibility of the modern world obtaining a realization of the new God. That God is not to be merely transcendent. He is to be immanent. If you will consider the nature of ideas, you will perceive that every discovery, every invention, every new idea, is in reality a miracle of inspiration. Out of the remote and obscure past, out of the ages of an-

29

tiquity, out of the race consciousness, our ideas pour in a stream. Then comes a new thought, a new idea, an invention, a discovery. Edisons arise. Lincolns take the lead. Columbus, Newton, the great brotherhood of those who have moved and advanced the world in its history. They are all revealing God to man. The prophets did the same in their way perhaps. But the new American God will have a wider range of prophets.

So far as the worship of Him is concerned, it will be felt and expressed not only in the great symbols of historic liturgies but in daily life, in the walks and ways of men. We do not say that it will be perfect. But it will be an advance. Faith, as it is called in religion, is, in secular terminology, Speculative Desire. Speculative Desire is the essential condition of human activity. The business man and the lover, the politician and the statesman, the scientist and the farmer, the inventor and the discoverer, the gambler and the moonshiner, the man about to be married and the man about to be divorced, the actor and

30

the artist, the bandit and the prize-fighter, the banker and the gold-brick man, the bull and the bear, the saint and the sinner, all alike are actuated by Speculative Desire, by Faith. In the language of the author of the Epistle to the Hebrews, a very ancient book, "Faith means we are confident of what we hope for, convinced of what we do not see." In short, we take a chance. People who do not take a chance never get anywhere. People who succeed want something. Their imagination works on it. They make a trial. It is the same in religion.

VI

The new God must be believed in. That is to say, there must be Speculative Desire for a knowledge of Him by everybody who expects to establish any relationship with Him. The chemist desires to produce a certain new and valuable compound. He speculates, illuminated by what knowledge he already possesses, about the reactions that will produce what he desires to

31

make. He dreams about it nights. Then he makes a trial. He puts his speculative theories to the test. If they work out, he has proved them. His test-tubes and solutions show the actual result. If he fails, he either tries again or gives up the attempt. In short, his test is pragmatic.

It is the same way with Faith. You conceive that there would be a value in making contact with the Source of all being and of all power. You would like to find yourself *en rapport* with Him. Very well. You speculate about His character and His laws. You realize that you must conform to them if you are to know Him as a reality. The result is a certain satisfaction, a peace, an assurance, an increased sense of illumination, a knowledge, an added power. You find that you are saved from your hells. You attain freedom from fear. There arises a definite experience of joy. You think in a new way. Brighter. There is contentment. You become permanently gay without the aid of a cocktail. It is really quite wonderful.

To be specific, suppose we consider one aspect of the new God, one of His essential attributes, one of the qualities that define and describe Him —Justice. Now, all jurists are agreed that Justice is an equilibrium of forces. Every shyster knows that this is true. The rich criminal can hold off the dogs of the law; the poor man has only a small chance. Might makes right. The big cannons always win. Perfectly true. Good philosophy. You do not find any balance between right and wrong in this world that even the least cynical can respect. But here comes in the Speculative Desire for a God of Justice, Who will weight the balance and give support to the weak but righteous cause. You have Faith that there is such a God. You speculate about the matter. You take into account the eternities. You scan the horizons of history. You study the sociological effect of intolerance, bigotry, dishonesty, crime, chicanery. You make a diagnosis of the psychology of the just and the unjust. You believe. You will make a trial, take a chance. *Fiat*

33

justitia ruat cœlum. You take your stand in the thin red line. You stick your hand into the slipping pulley. You are crushed. *Soit.* At the very moment you hear the chants of the choirs of heaven and the Voice of God:

> When sudden—how think ye, the end?
> Did I say "without friend"?
> Say rather, from marge to blue marge
> The whole sky grew his targe
> With the sun's self for visible boss,
> While an arm ran across
> Which the earth heaved beneath like a breast
> Where the wretch was safe pressed!
> Do you see? Just my vengeance complete,
> The man sprang to his feet,
> Stood erect, caught at God's skirts, and prayed!
> —So, I was afraid!

And the new American God will be the God of Truth. Justice merges into Truth. If your Speculative Desire conceives of Truth as something to be realized, something to be expressed, something to be coöperated with, you are al-

34

ready an initiate in the true religion. You have joined the Church Militant. You have entered the real Salvation Army. In spite of the flapdoodle of fools, the lies of lawyers, the phantasies of philosophers, the tangled trickery of theologians, the ugly untruths of uplifters, the falsehoods of Fundamentalists, the preposterous prevarications of Prohibitionists, the silly solecisms of Socialists, the conspiracies of corporations and capitalists, the hypocrisies of holier-than-thou hierophants, the fictions of fanatics, the elusive, eclectic, empirical exaggerations of ecclesiastics, the arrogant and artful arguments of Authority, you still believe. Your desire for Truth and your speculative enthusiasm compel you to feel that you can clean up the nasty mess. You become an Apostle of the new God, the God of Truth. *Magna est veritas et prævalebit.* (A little jaded Latin comports with your theological mind.) You take up the Cross, and if you see a head, you hit it. Good for you! That is the true crusade for the votaries of the new American God.

35

The congregation will now sing three stanzas of the wonderful old hymn, "We march, we march to victory," to the honor and glory of that God. You have disentangled the Truth. You have seen Him face to face. You lift up your heart. *Sursum corda.* You are now a worshiper. *Hosanna!*

And Beauty. Beauty, perhaps more than any other attribute, needs to be stressed. For the old Gods of this country are notoriously ugly. Their hideous temples deface the landscape on every hand. The Puritanical idolaters have constructed a God that hates color, grace and taste. They worship Him in their drab tabernacles with hideous sounds, roaring organs, and psalms sung through their noses. They think of beauty as the creation of the Devil. Vestments, lights, colors, incense, the splendor of ceremonial, the delicacy of storied windows, the mystery of vast naves, such things they abhor. Their chief act of worship consists of listening to a stupid man deliver a dull address. Their priests wear frock coats and look like undertakers. If one has any Specu-

36

lative Desire in relation to the God of Beauty, one goes out into the great cathedral of Nature and worships Him in the stars, in the splendor of the sunset, in the pale blue of distant mountain ranges, in the restless turmoil of the green sea; one finds Him in the delicate beauty of flowers, in the shimmer and flash of gems, in the exquisite grace of the human form, in the divine perfection of the human face; or it may be that He speaks to one out of the sonorous cadences of the Seventh Symphony of Beethoven, or looks out from a canvas by Botticelli. Nature is the Great Artist's own building, His church. Art is His *métier*. The man who has any Speculative Desire about Beauty, either as it is found in nature or reproduced by genius, will believe in the new God. And the person who works in the element of Beauty, whether professionally or not, knows something of the Eternal Creative Spirit in a very close and intimate companionship, indeed.

These are a few of the features of the new

37

American God. They have not lacked recognition, at times, in the past. God has not left Himself altogether without witness in any age or in any place. What America needs is simply a more perfect realization of the possibilities of a determined faith in the One True God.

If you ask me about the name for this new American God, my idea is that it is probably better just to keep the old word for Him, and call Him simply God. Honestly, I think it would scarcely be worth while to change the name.

FROM AUTHORITY TO EXPERIENCE

I

AT a church dinner. A very fashionable church dinner. Distinguished laymen in evening dress. Aristocratic ladies in jewelry and colors. Bishops and ecclesiastical dignitaries in swallow-tails and silk waistcoats. An orchestra and choir in the gallery for the music. Costly food and a profusion of exotic flowers. But, being a church dinner, no wine. No visible cocktails. Speeches, of course. That is the chief purpose of church dinners. Something ulterior.

"It is quite time," began the bishop, "that these disturbing speculations were laid aside and we returned to the recognition of properly constituted authority."

"It is not surprising," replied the dean, "that the whole religious world is in a state of turmoil. It will continue. We are in a period of transition from authority to experience."

The lady across the table puffed learnedly at her cigarette. The laymen tried to appear interested and understanding. Two clergymen of austere aspect frowned like Torquemada at the examination of a heretic before the Holy Office. A third cleric grinned as a secretary grins when he hears that the Cause has been mentioned in a will. A distinct thrill went through the great ballroom. The keynote of a situation had been struck.

It has long been the feeling that there is the sound of a going in the treetops of the religious world, but the exact nature of the period as an historical movement has perhaps never been phrased so accurately as the dean on this occasion put it.

"From authority to experience." It is happening in every other aspect of human life, in the political, social, scientific fields. The history of the modern world is made up of just such tran-

40

sitions all along the line. The individual equally goes through such transition. The boy graduating from school, leaving home, passes out of the control of such authoritative influences as he has been forced unwillingly to recognize into the light of experiences where he must stand as an individual on his own. Why should religion be excepted from the general order?

Evidently the dean had sounded a tocsin. The bell had rung. The little beam of the candle was shimmering from the church steeple. Rebellion had raised its head. Revolution was in the air. The word was "Give me liberty, or give me death." Signals were flashing. Matches were ready for the cannon. The movement of muffled feet could be heard.

II

It is said that Junípero Serra, the Spanish friar who built so many of those charming old missions you visit when you go to California, did not understand a word of the language of the Indians to whom he had been sent as a missionary. He had, nevertheless, three sermons. His first sermon consisted of striking himself on the chest with his fists. If that failed to make converts, Junípero produced a scourge, such as monks use, from the folds of his habit, raised his robes, and beat himself on his bare buttocks after the manner of the flagellants. If the savage heart was still untouched, the forceful friar seized a jagged stone of great size and, baring his bosom, pounded his flesh until the blood ran down in streams. Invariably this last appeal convinced the gainsayers.

"Ugh!" said the braves. "Great medicine!" And straightway the tribe submitted to the authority of Holy Church. It is a source of wonder to the traveler in Central and South America to find how thoroughly the Spaniard gave his language and his religion to the aborigines of his far-flung colonial empire after the conquistadores. Authority was there established under the

42

flaming torch of the Inquisition. The *auto da fé* lasted down well into the nineteenth century— almost to the time of the auto-da-Ford. Early settlers have told me of attending mass with Indian congregations, and of the ceaseless beating of the tom-tom and the wild monotonous droning of the worshipers during the sacred mysteries. I know places in the Andes—but of that another time.

An analysis of the basis upon which religious authority is accepted will convince you that it is a basis of emotion. The psychologists have been telling us that all ideas derive from emotion and that emotion derives from sensation. In the case of Junípero's Indian converts the course is apparent. They saw, they were moved, they believed. What they believed was for the immediate purpose comparatively unimportant. No doubt, the good friars taught them many things later on.

Where religion is established the acceptance of religious authority is generally a part of one's group psychology, but in order to maintain itself authority must continually be reëstablished over the individual by appeals to his emotional nature. It has always been so.

Ignatius Loyola, founder of the Jesuit order, wrote a slight but very important little book called "Manresa." The principles of this book are recognized by students of the subject as fundamental to the whole authoritative devotional fabric of the Catholic Church. Ignatius was a man of analytical mind of the highest order. In his book he anticipated some of the discoveries of modern physiological psychology by three hundred years. In dealing with religious meditation or contemplation Ignatius directs "the application of the senses." Sight, touch, hearing,—if possible, even taste and smell,— must be employed to arouse the emotions of the neophyte, who, deeply moved, becomes submissive. To the same effect, and with the best motives in the world, St. Francis invented the Christmas crib and St. Dominic devised the fifteen

44

chaplets of the rosary. The Stations of the Cross is another instance. In fact, all the devices of art, architecture, painting, sculpture, music, ritual, lights, and vestments produce and are intended to produce just those emotions that will make the believer accept religious authority, support the institution, and perform works of virtue in the cause of religion. This is not an arraignment; it is an explanation.

Protestantism, breaking from the established authority of the Mediæval Church, naturally swept out the instruments by which that authority was sustained. It declared them to be "superstitious." But it now finds itself without the means of maintaining its own authority. It relied merely upon the reading of the Bible and the preaching of the minister. The Bible in the vernacular was then new and passed without criticism as final. Preaching was fervid, controversial, negative. But Biblical criticism and the paucity of eloquent preachers have forced Protestantism to turn back at least to stained glass

45

and such music as it can produce, as aids in a failing cause. Protestant authority, so far as the laity is concerned, is to-day practically nil. It is only where some perfervid evangelist can establish, through his emotional appeals, a temporary submission that there is even the semblance of it. Where Protestantism is stable, that is due, with few exceptions, to group consciousness and endowments or the support of rich individuals.

The eye is the organ most immediately connected with the imagination centers of the brain. Protestantism swept out of the churches everything interesting to look at and depended upon the ear. Moving pictures and psychology were unknown when Protestantism was born. If they had been known, our ancestors might not have made so prodigious a mistake. As for Protestant music, it is devotionally good as a general rule only when it is taken over from some Catholic composer. And as for Protestant stained glass, with few exceptions it will produce emo-

46

tions all right, but they are scarcely of a strictly religious character. "Brighten the Corner" and "The Brewer's Big Horses Can't Run Over Me" were excellent for arousing the emotions of the Billy Sunday crowds. But they have failed to hold their vogue. It is significant that for over forty years there has not been produced a single religious musical composition, Catholic or Protestant, that has a notable popular appeal. Why?

III

The reasons, then, for the break-down of authority both in the Anglican Church and in Protestant churches generally are not far to seek. Certain of them are affecting Roman Catholicism as well. For in the present age there has come upon the world a conception that affects the imagination of multitudes, raising doubts as to the validity of formerly accepted emotions and stirring human feeling to a high degree. Intellectually we have only recently emerged from the Middle Ages. For years the very seats of learning, our colleges and universities themselves, lived in the past, looking backward to classical antiquity as a seated mistress of all learning, accepting the dicta of the age of Aristotle or of Cicero as authoritative and final. Our fathers were trained to look backward to the golden past. Youth today looks forward. Even our colleges are beginning to do the same.

There is no need to discuss the change in the cosmic outlook. The magazines have been full of the effect upon religious conceptions of the new view of the universe, of man's insignificance, of the long ages of the creative process, of the absurdity of an anthropomorphic conception of God. It is old stuff. But while these things have been known and recognized by the educated for generations, we have probably not counted upon the power of the race inheritance, the delayed acceptance into the popular imagination of a geocentric cosmography. After all, the religious masses have just begun to realize that

48

the planet floats a speck in the great voids. As this idea is visualized and takes possession of the mind, it creates impressions that obtrude upon the old religious imagery.

> There's a home for little children
> Above the bright blue sky

may still do for children. It revolts the college boy or girl. And so do most of the hymns in the hymn-book. They were written in a past age when men saw their place in the universe as the men of fifty thousand years ago saw it.

The theology that was behind the devotional machinery of the church comes into question in exact ratio as general knowledge increases. The pictures that thrilled the souls of believers in the Incarnation, the Redemption, the Ascension, and Session at the right hand of God have to be reconstructed to fit the facts. They were crude and mediæval in outline and coloring and must needs be done over in modern dress. Until they are so done over most thinking people put them on the shelf—though I have met men, educated men, who tell me that they still manage to keep their religion and their science in two separate compartments, living in one compartment for a single hour on Sundays and in the other compartment all the rest of the week. On Sunday they maintain that God made the world in six literal days; on Monday they are evolutionists. This accomplishment is really quite common. I have been wondering whether it may not extend also to morals. In a period of revolutionary transition one must expect strange compromises.

But if the period of transition from authority to experience has grotesque aspects, it is not without its tragic side. "Easter," said a woman to me recently,—she had just lost a child,— "Easter must be lovely in Heaven." We cannot so easily slip the moorings of ancient prepossessions without the sense of a vast loss—unless our experience has itself been developed.

At the present moment an enormous number of people stand at the crossroads. They have scrapped the authority of churches, they have no regard for ecclesiastical organization. But neither have they any actual spiritual experience to supply the empty soul. They want something to take the place of that which they have lost. Interest in religion was never greater. The sociological value of it is recognized by all public men. Presidents and statesmen, editors and professors, college presidents and millionaires, dramatists and novelists, all talk and write about religion. At the luncheons of the Kiwanis and Rotary clubs nothing brings greater applause than a boost of religion. If a minister makes a speech at one of their meetings, they cheer him to the echo, pat him on the back, and sing,

> How do ye do, Mr. Doodle,
> How do ye doodle, doodle, do?"

But a careful survey shows that very few of the men who stress the social value of religion at public meetings are regular attendants at church. When Sunday comes they play golf.

51

IV

What, then, is the experience toward which the world is moving?

I think that the transition is very largely a matter of emphasis and interpretation. Authoritative religion has been the mother of so much splendid virtue and magnificent heroism in the past that no one would lightly thrust it all aside as worthless. Its values must be retained and expanded rather. The one thing that is perfectly clear is that in any conflict between arbitrary dogma, whether Biblical or ecclesiastical, and the established facts of science men will invariably and justly give the preference to the latter. It is only peasants and the undeveloped mind of childhood that can any longer be imposed upon. It has long been recognized by the theologues themselves that such doctrines as rest upon the Biblical account of creation and the fall of man, though still preached at Dayton and to the hill-billies of the remote mountain districts, are regarded by the educated as mere poetical folk-fore. The transition on this line may be said to be already accomplished. All of the Old Testament, in fact, apart from the moral and spiritual values enshrined there, has no bearing upon the religion of the modern man. Its legends and history may have a mystical interpretation, but they no longer inhibit the advance of knowledge. Politicians, candidates for Congress, on the lookout for the votes of clodhoppers, men of the Bryan-Upshaw type, may profess to accept the Bible from "kiver to kiver" as a final book of science, but nobody else does, surely.

Matters of this sort were settled by scholars a generation ago. The learned of the present day are shifting their polemic to problems like the origin and character of the eschatology of Jesus, the authenticity of the New Testament, the question of interpolations, especially in regard to the sacraments and the church, the amount early Christianity borrowed from the pagan mysteries, the philosophical background for the dogmatic definitions of the ecumenical councils. There can be no doubt that the outcome of study on these and kindred lines will parallel the work done on Old Testament criticism. But in spite of our greatly increased means of communication, the extent of education, and the enormous interest, it takes a good many years for ideas to filter down to and affect the imagination of the masses. Add to this the opposition of obscurantists, the brayings of ignorance, the crotchets of cranks, the ingrained prejudices of official old women, the thought grooves of narrow-minded bigots, the stupidity of settled pastors, the solemn asseverations of popular preachers, the deliberate policy of press-agented prelates who design to keep the masses in ignorance, and you might think that the transition would be slow. It is slow, but it moves.

I hold no brief for Christian Science, New Thought, Mental Science, Pastor Russell or the rest. The Vedantic and Buddhist missions in

New York do not interest me greatly. Mr. Sinnett, Madame Blavatsky, and Mrs. Besant, with their new avatars, have not swayed me very much. But all these have done something to further the movement of a transition from authority to experience and they have affected the trend of Christian devotion quite definitely. Multitudes have gone out of the churches recently to seek a new experience in devotional emotion which does not lead to the acceptance of ecclesiastical authority. And multitudes who still remain in the churches have shifted their conceptions of spiritual values.

Consider, for instance, the transition as it affects the idea of the Christian virtue known (to some) as humility. In the "Manresa" of St. Ignatius, to which I have already referred, there is an exercise on humility. The saintly author gives three degrees of humility. He says:—

The first degree of humility consists in perfect submission to the law of God, so that we should be ready

55

to refuse the empire of the whole world, or even sacrifice our lives, rather than willingly transgress any precept which obliges under pain of mortal sin.

The second degree is more perfect; it consists in the indifference of the soul toward riches or poverty, honor or shame, health or sickness, provided the glory of God and salvation are equally secured on both sides.

The third degree is the highest degree of Christian perfection. It consists of preferring, for the sole love of Jesus Christ and for the wish to resemble Him more, poverty to riches, shame to honor, sickness to health, and so forth, even if on both sides your salvation and the glory of God were equally to be found.

This may be heroic, but it is not common sense. The whole drift and tendency of the race is and always has been toward life, toward livingness, toward health, wealth, and happiness. No modern interpretation of the sayings of Jesus would find even the first degree of St. Ignatius in the Gospel. Jesus said, "I am come that they might have life, and that they might have it more abundantly."

A new conception of the virtue of humility,

then, is arising. It does not consist in accepting arbitrary ecclesiastical authority as the assured law of God. Neither does it lie in depreciating your own knowledge, ability, or powers. Nor least of all does it seek miseries that can be avoided, and a whining pose like that of *Uriah Heep*. Humility in essence is merely the recognition of the truth. Your actual limitations, your real ignorance, your dependence for all that you are and all that you have upon the supreme power that gives life—that is humility. To remember these limitations and this power constantly is the art of the virtue. Humility may coexist with the loftiest claims and the most outspoken and courageous egoism, if that egoism is justified. Jesus did not come merely to die. He came with convictions and bold utterance, an egoism such as the world had never heard before. "I am the way, and the truth, and the life: no man cometh unto the Father, but by me." When regarding his humanity by itself, Jesus said, "I can of mine own self do nothing."

57

But realizing the divine omnipotence within, he said, "All power is given unto me in heaven and in earth."

Another shift in interpretation and emphasis in this period of transition from authority to experience is found in relation to the idea of the kingdom of Heaven. It was formerly taught quite generally by Catholic and Protestants alike that the kingdom of God on earth was the Church and that the kingdom of God in Heaven could be experienced only after death. Twenty years ago the pink socialists and guild brethren who clung to religion began to teach that the kingdom would be realized when their theories had been accepted, when Prohibition was voted for, when capitalism fell—a kingdom in which paid secretaries would sit on golden thrones, sniffing incense and giving directions. Alas! the war and Russia put a crimp in it. But there may be something more in the present emphasis of the sayings of Jesus, that the kingdom is right here now, at hand; that it is not visible, cometh not with

58

observation; that it is within us. It is in this direction that experience is taking the place of authority among those who are interested in religion if not in ecclesiastical organization.

There are many other aspects of the matter. It would be of interest, if space permitted, to pursue the problem into the conception of God —God as creative energy. God in relation to locality, God in relation to human consciousness. What is God? Where is God? These are questions that religious experience above all things seeks to answer. For upon the answers depends the tendency of modern religion.

Everybody understands the difference between moonlight and sunshine. One is reflected and secondary; the other is inherent. And if you will consider the difference between the teachings of Jesus and the teachings about Jesus, the ancient theology and the mystery of an actual consciousness of the divine in human life, you will perceive the real essence of the transformation of authority into experience.

The impregnated cell out of which the human body is developed has no brain, no evidence of the power of reason. It grows, fissiparous in structure, selecting the chemical elements that form the body through the mysterious power of an instinctive emotional wisdom. Ultimately it develops a brain. The brain, kindling consciousness out of feeling, forms thought. At a time the mind of man looks back upon the origin of its own formation and perceives the presence of a wisdom and power within from which all has come. "The kingdom of God is within you."

"How to the singer cometh the song?" sings Walt Whitman. And when one considers the origin of ideas, of inventions, of discoveries, the growth of civilization, the knowledge of laws and of arts, the poems written, the pictures painted, the cities created, the business and order of the world of nations, whether you call the origin creative energy or call it God, you have a religious experience that Augustine, Francis, Eckhart, Teresa, John of the Cross, Plotinus, or

the mystics of the East could not deny. It may
not produce the stigmata, but it will give you
the joy of life. You are no longer in the moonlight of the experiences of others in relation to
the divine. You have entered the sunshine of
reality.

V

Religious authority, like the mediæval mind,
looks always backward, toward the past. Its
wisdom, its mysteries, its experience with God,
its miracles, its revelations, all took place centuries ago. It has held the world of thought in
thrall for two thousand years. But if God is the
creative and controlling power of the universe,
why confine His operations to the first few
years of the Christian era? If there is a con-
tinuous unfolding of the secrets of the universe
to the mind of man, is there not equally a con-
tinuous revelation of the nature of God? If
miracles ever happened, why should they not

61

be happening now? Is truth confined to the studies of Augustine, Jerome, Basil, Hilary, Gregory, Chrysostom, the fathers of Nice, Ephesus, Constantinople, Calcedon, the traditions of the first six centuries? Excellent men and excellent traditions, no doubt. But has not this vast array of ecclesiastical authority been used as a blanket to stifle thought? A little freedom, good masters, from the fulminations of the theologues of the orthodox schools. Let us think out of the interpretations for ourselves, untrammeled and *de novo*. Let us breathe the fresh air of this new morning without forever smelling the dust of obsolete libraries. God is not confined to old books. Neither is He shut up in churches.

The most enormous religious ceremony, or series of ceremonies, in all history has just been staged by the Roman Catholic hierarchy in that most wicked city in the world, Chicago. The newspaper accounts of processions and masses, of vast crowds of pilgrims, numbering hundreds of thousands, of a scarlet Pullman train for the cardinals, of public streets decorated with columns of white and gold draped in laurel and surmounted by bronze eagles, of choirs numbering sixty thousand voices, of the ceremony on the lake front and at the new town of Mundelein, of the papal legate, the fifteen princes of the church, archbishops and bishops, mitred abbots and abbots, monsignori, papal chamberlains and knights,

> Priest, doctor, hermit, monk grown white
> With prayer, the broken-hearted nun,
> The martyr, the wan acolyte,
> The incense-swinging child . . .

bewilder the imagination and—make for authority. It has been a demonstration in force.

There is nothing in the way of similar exhibitions that can compare in dramatic effect, in poetry, in color and variety, with a well-arranged religious procession. The Elks and the Tall Cedars pale into insignificance before it;

even the Knights Templars look like the wooden soldiers of the "Chauve-Souris" in comparison. Moreover, it stands for a very high ideal, something beyond the mere parade in unwonted costumes that seems somehow to meet a need of human nature. No one can doubt the sincerity and piety of the vast numbers of laity participating. Their thought undoubtedly was *ad majorem Dei gloriam.*

But unprejudiced and intelligent people will nevertheless ask to what spiritual values, to what experience, this great and well-oiled enterprise leads? Does it mean *au fond* much more than a demand for submission of the intellect to an established and settled hierarchy? Is its purpose any different from that of Junípero Serra with the Indians? If so, what increase of knowledge, insight, and character will be assured by joining the procession? It may be an ecclesiastical accomplishment to understand the meaning of terms like *mozetta, biretta, zucchetto,* and to know the proper occasion for wearing a *cappa magna,* but will this throw any light upon the grim questions of eternity, upon the unsolved problems of survival after death? Is there any assurance that God will be found at the end of the rainbow? Liberty for the intellect has only lately been wrung, at much cost of blood and treasure, from just such authoritative and imposing ceremonial dominance. Spectacular pomp is not an answer.

Or, is it a conceivable thing that the Roman Church now desires by this splendid show in the New World to make a gesture of tolerance to modern thought and ascertained knowledge, extending the poetic beauty and religious mystery of its ancient faith to such as may feel that experience is not only a costly but an incomplete teacher? Has its own experience something still to contribute to a world which yet lies in darkness and in the shadow of death?

RELIGIO AMERICANA

I

AT the Château de Blois in Trois Rivières I met the organ builder from St. Sulpice. A most agreeable man. It must be admitted that he wore when I first saw him a slight *morgue*. This was doubtless due to the emanations. For the Château de Blois is half sanatorium, half hotel. The mineral springs which bubble up into the baths and drinking fountains give off a most pungent aroma, sulphurous and mephitic. And mingled with this are the odors of stale vintages left in the glasses of relays of thirsty American tourists, who invariably pause here in their fifty-mile-an-hour flight down the St. Lawrence Valley for refreshment, together with the penetrating fumes of the French cuisine. A stuffy place devoid of fresh air for the benefit of the invalids who can be seen walking about in bath-robes with their attendants.

It was quite natural that the organ-builder should begin the conversation with a reference to the value of incense in public worship.

"It must be admitted, monsieur," said he in a French that contained no trace of the Canadian patois, "that incense is very valuable in the service of religion. In a crowded church without ventilation I have known some congregations of peasants to resemble in point of odor a herd of wet dogs. The incense is very serviceable on such occasions. I have read somewhere that it was originally used for the purpose of sanitation, a disinfectant."

"That may be so," he hastened to add. "But I would not have you suppose that only for this reason do I value it. Not at all, monsieur. It is also a most beautiful symbol of prayer. What could be more exquisite? The smoke from the thurible ascending up to heaven typical of the rising prayers of the priest and people, round-

ing out their imperfection? Acceptable to God.
And very Biblical, monsieur. You find it in the
Bible as well as in the traditional usage of the
Church from the earliest ages. And consider also
this, monsieur. A man who is blind may be
able to content himself at the mass with what he
can hear. But a man who is both blind and deaf,
what can he find in the assistance at mass except
the satisfaction of the smell? Our holy Mother,
the Church, is very considerate of her children,
monsieur."

"Now Protestantism," he continued, "has little
to offer to a man who is even deaf. It would not
matter much, if he were blind. There is little to
see in its churches. But if he cannot hear either
the music or the sermon, what advantage is there
in his attendance? None, monsieur. Is it not so?"

"You are, then," I ventured, "devoted to your
church?"

"But naturally, monsieur," he replied, "I am
a good Catholic. It is, in fact, my custom to
assist at mass every day. It is an inspiration.

I find God there. When I go into a Catholic church and see the little red light flickering before the altar, then I know that God is there, the Real Presence. I can talk to Him and He talks to me."

"The Roman Catholic Church," I asked, changing the subject slightly from what seemed a bit mystical and *intime*, "is very strong in Canada?"

"In French Canada," he replied, "practically everybody is Catholic. The Church is the ruling power. Others may, of course, be permitted to have their services, but they are negligible. Did you observe, for example, the Methodist building here in Trois Rivières? So small, so deserted? And what excellent result this uniformity of religion has! A contented and peaceful people, monsieur. Slight occasion for the police. For the influence of the clergy is everywhere felt."

"The workmen in your factory," I suggested, "they also are religious?"

"Most assuredly," he answered. "And they

are content. If a man has divine things, he wants but little here below. There are never any strikes with us."

II

Every American traveler knows the superb Château Frontenac in Quebec. The magnificent building towers above a city which vies in picturesque quality with Edinburgh, Naples or Palermo. The wide river at its base flows off to the distant sea and the Heights of Abraham near-by tell their historic story. It was there I met the hundred per cent. American. He was a business man from the States. In the lobby were streams of youth and beauty, the styles of Fifth Avenue, a parade before afternoon tea.

"Hear those girls speak French?" asked the hundred per cent. American. "They look enough like the girls at home to make you think they'd have better sense than to jabber a lingo that nobody can understand. But I did learn one word of the jargon since I came up here. Say, did you know what *école* means? It means *school*. I found that out from the auto signs along the road. Yes sir; *school*. They put a sign along the road before every school and the word is *école*. And would you believe it? Every one of the schools has a big cross on top. Yes, sir; a cross. They're all Catholics here. Churches, churches everywhere. And licker. Licker sold in government stores! Think of it! And not a bad idea either. Rather a relief not to be having to sneak it in as we do over the border."

"No; I haven't seen any drunks," he continued in answer to my question. "But, say, this country is a paradise for the priests. God conducts the only big business in this country. That is, if you cut out the tourist business. In every little village we came through the church was the big smoke. Enormous structures. And the priest's house was always the best house in town. They live well, those fellows."

"I couldn't help thinking," he went on, "what

71

kind of a time a man who was a Methodist, or a Baptist, or a Holy Roller would have, if he tried to break into the business game up in these parts. I reckon he'd go to the wall mighty quick, unless he changed his religion and got down and kowtowed to the priests. Yes, sir; one religion, everybody in it and the chief business of the country."

A renewal of refreshment at this point enabled him to continue.

"But, of course, this ain't real religion. Plumb idolatry, I call it. Did you see all those idols at Sainte Anne de Beaupré? Did you see those stairs where people crawl up on their knees? Well, sir; they make a regular business of burning down the shrine there every so often to keep the money coming in for a new building. Shrewd, I'll say it is! I'm goin' to tell my wife's pastor when I get back home to send up some missionaries here to convert these people. Real heathens, worse than the savages the Woman's Missionary Society is always sewing for back

72

home. We Methodists ought to take the thing up in a big way and convert these people."

"At home, then," I put in, "you are an active member of the church?"

"Well, that's perhaps too much to say," he answered. "I belong. I pay my shot. And I'm on some of the boards. But I can't say that I go to church much. In our town, among the men, they don't ask so much what church do you go to as what church supper do you attend. The women folks do set up the best church suppers! Of course, the Catholics down there are the only people who go much to church. Afraid of the priests, you know. Those Catholics seem to be getting in on everything in America nowadays. I see where they're trying to run Smith in as the next President. I can't understand it. And all those vestments and queer ceremonies, incense, candles, bells, and, all that sort of hokum. What's the world coming to?"

"But at the lodge—" I began.

"Oh, at the lodge," he interrupted, "that's a

different proposition. It doesn't mean anything there. We wear all kinds of dewdabs. Looks rather pretty, I think. But seriously, what does get my goat is these here preachers who criticize the Bible. I don't understand all this talk about evolution that's going on. The Bible, just as it is, is good enough for me. What do these fellows mean by teaching that men are descended from monkeys? Religion is the most important thing in life. What would become of the country, as President Coolidge says, if we did not have religion? It ought to be taught in the public schools and there ought to be a law passed to stop all this talk about evolution. I'd put some of these preachers that I hear talk over the radio on Sundays in jail, if I had my way."

III

In the United States there is nothing quite comparable to the condition of ecclesiastical Canada in the Province of Quebec. There are

74

approximations. Utah and its Mormons, the Baptist régime in the Bible Belt of the South, Scandinavian Lutherans in the Northwest, German Lutherans in the Middle West, Irish Roman Catholics in a thousand municipalities all over the land. But nothing quite so neat, quite so thorough. Not but what the aspiration is all there, Even the effort. Witness the notorious Methodist propaganda in Washington. They would all run the world, if they could. Especially the clergy, the ministers, the priests and prelates. Not for the lust of power. Of course. No, no, never. Merely to see to it that God, His laws, His ministers, receive due respect. Impersonal and detached. Only it happens that to them has been intrusted the mission of directing the conduct and the consciences of mankind. Thus they go as far as they are able. And the only thing that stops them is the opposition of another equally ambitious and determined group—or the supercilious smiles of that great and growing multitude of those who seldom go to church.

When they can manage to combine, they are sufficiently terrible. They put over laws with claws.

There are in the United States some 165 listed sects of religion and more than forty unlisted sects of religion; roughly speaking, therefore about two hundred different religious bodies. The divisions follow for the most part racial lines. The various strata of immigrants, that is to say, brought with their bundles of household goods the lares and penates of their household gods. All the old divisive prejudices, the peculiarities, the customs and habits of devotion, the *odium theologicum* of the race inheritance came along. And in the face of an alien civilization these were either intensified in the determination for survival or they were entirely lost in the contact with educational influences in a civilization which, so far as the immigrants themselves were concerned, was higher than that to which they had access at home. Less than half of our citizens at the present time are religious in the sense that they are affiliated with any religious body whatever. This is perhaps a higher percentage than existed in colonial days when conditions on the seaboard, contrasted with conditions in the Old World, made it easy for the colonists to drop their religions. The eighteenth century was very irreligious. Freedom from authority was in the air.

The theoretical separation of church and state in this country permits easily the varieties of religious opinion and the organization of any new sect. This separation has been regarded as one of the greatest contributions of our republic to the advance of civilization. Perhaps it is. But it is also an unmistakable cause of the delay in amalgamation and unification of the nation. Religious differences are the strongest influence in keeping the race groups apart. In America it is common to find adult men and women born in this country who do not speak English. They have been brought up and educated, carried through school and college, launched into business, and live all their lives exactly as their parents lived

77

in Germany, Holland, Scandinavia, Greece, Palestine, Hungary, Russia, and a dozen other countries, so far as the linguistic and cultural features of the United States are concerned. Their religion is the chief factor in maintaining a paramount loyalty to the land of their fathers. There has to be a considerable breakdown of the inherited and inculcated prejudices before Abie can marry his Irish Rose or the rabbi will eat his ham sandwich. As a more general rule, Abie marries only Rebecca, Rose marries Patrick, and the priest and the rabbi never even meet.

Within even the best and most liberal of these religious sects the members tend to become a little world by themselves, a whispering gallery, a close corporation. They know only the names of their own divines, the condition of their own churches. It is only that the country is still large enough to lose them in remote localities or because our people of the greater majority are sufficiently liberal, tolerant, and gifted with

78

a sense of humor, that no national trouble is encountered—except in case of war—with these alien religious groups. But it does not tend toward nationality to have Greek disputes of royalists and Venezelists, or Irish disputes of the Free State, or Italian disputes about Mussolini, fought out on American soil. Even now we are compelled to call in the police from time to time. It may be that in some future crisis the methods of the Roman emperors for the settling of religious disputes may have to be invoked. The separation of church and state has never been found easy in the past. And when it is not the state that encroaches on the liberties of the church, it is the church that provokes reprisals by its interference with the state. The American experiment is not yet an assured success.

IV

The divisions of religion in this country, it is felt by many, are the greatest weakness to the

79

cause of all religion. The resultant confusion in spiritual and moral ideals especially among the young throughout the nation tend to loosen the hold of multitudes upon any and all spiritual and moral ideals. It is difficult for religion to be presented with the imposing effect that the conception of it warrants. Worship on a majestic scale becomes impossible. The economic result of the need of maintaining such a heterogeneous mass of organizations with the overhead of officialdom and innumerable buildings, is wasteful and extravagant. The rivalry and strife between the sects is discreditable.

And beyond question the differences between many, especially of the so-called Evangelical sects, is merely of terminology. Their ancient theological definitions are worn threadbare and scarcely even exist in the minds of most of the laity. It might be thought that there could be at least some degree of unity arranged between them. But the curious tenacity of racial strains and social differences, combined with a determined spirit of independence always fostered by the clerical class, serve to keep them apart. Unity of organization implies at least some degree of order, control, restriction, subordination, authority. And these things certain religious bodies and groups particularly hate. In fact, certain of the most influential of the Protestant bodies are purely congregational in polity. They are known by the same name but have no central controlling authority. Each parochial body is practically a separate sect. The Jews, the Baptists, and the Congregationalists are united merely by name, by racial sympathy, and a general consensus of ideas. They have not and would resent any other kind of unity. And many other religious groups are almost as loosely organized.

The spirit of American Protestantism was born in opposition to religious authority. Its trend is towards independence and individualism. It is naturally suspicious of the monarchical system of episcopacy and all hierarchical

81

organization. It would require great economic pressure and state insistence to move it in the direction of united order. The hundred per cent. American sits lightly in his ecclesiastical relationships. If anything goes contrary to his ideas, if the preacher says anything that he does not approve of, he easily leaves his church and goes to another or stays away altogether from the observance of religion in public. And he feels that he is doing the right thing. He will not support that of which he does not entirely approve. And his judgment is final. Moreover, he can always find those who will agree with him and endorse his stand. Submission is a virtue which he does not understand.

Now the reasons for this attitude in American Protestantism become apparent when we study the present disputes between the so-called Modernists and the Fundamentalists. Modernism in America means the attempt among the more educated leaders of religion in this country to make a synthesis between received religion and edu-

cation. Fundamentalism accepts the authority of
the Bible, the church, the pope, as final and em-
ploys education merely to justify such acceptance. Modernism is critical. Fundamentalism is
apologetic. Modernism places ascertained truth
above authority. Fundamentalism holds that religious authority is ultimate truth and that whatever seems contrary to it can be explained away
or is an error of fact. The American system
of education, therefore, has been the foe of religious authority. Jews, Roman Catholics, and
many of the Protestant sects have on this account
strained every effort to keep their children under
their own systems of education, wherein religious authority would be sustained by every
weapon of the pleader and the apologist and the
facts of science made to conform to this standard. In this respect the Roman Catholics alone
have had any measure of success on a large
scale. The others have yielded to secular influences and to the advantages of secular support.
For the funds to sustain education have come

mostly from the state or from individuals who, being rich, were not dominated by religious authority. And no country in the world affords such opportunities for education as America.

The real strife, then, among educated, or partially educated, Americans is not along the lines of the Reformation settlements. These are obsolescent and relegated to the snarling groups of illiterate peasants in the remote hinterlands of thought. The strife is between religious authority of whatever kind and freedom of thought, whether truth is to be accepted on a basis of intrinsic validity or on a basis of faith in prescription. The clamor of this battle is all around us. The freethinkers are by no means adverse to religion; many of them are very religious. But at the present time there is no armistice in sight between the opposing forces. The drift is, on the one hand, towards sheer individualism and, on the other, towards the Roman pontiff. For those who incline to the acceptance of religious authority feel that there is really no reason for stopping short of a goal that has been so efficacious for so many centuries and has had the experience of ages in ecclesiastical domination. But the general drift is away from authority.

V

The really deep line of cleavage in religious America, however, is between Protestantism and Catholicism. This is both racial and religious. It runs all through our social and political life. The Celtic and Latin groups in our civilization are far removed in many respects from the primitive strains of Anglo-Saxon and the later Teutonic and Scandinavian layers of immigration in this country. The two classes divergent in religion do not touch or mingle closely. In many municipalities, it is true, the Irish dominate the political situation. That is because the more able groups are engaged in business and eschew politics. In a few communities in the

85

greater cities of the country old Roman Catholic families have high social standing. But these are few. Apart from the political prestige in municipal politics, the Protestant elements are more dominant as they are more numerous. And the line of separation is marked by the religious difference.

On the part of Protestants the antipathy to Roman Catholicism amounts to a fear complex. Deep down in the racial consciousness there is the memory of ecclesiastical autocracy, the fires of the Inquisition, the thumb-screw, and the rack. A Protestant is apt to become uneasy at the very sight of a crucifix. Incense, candles, ceremonial, in connection with religion, grate on his nerves. They have, as the hundred per cent. American at the Château Frontenac observed, a meaning. They arouse prejudice and passion. He beholds in them the thin edge of the wedge. Four hundred years of cultivated and habitual antipathy survive within him. He may know some excellent individual Roman Catholics as friends, but he does not quite trust them. They seem to him to harbor some profound ulterior motive behind and beyond all their friendship that may deliver them over to the Pope. It is a curious and dreadful obsession. But it is very real. The results are manifest.

Protestants can manage to get together, for example, in many of their social and most of their charitable enterprises, in education especially. But there is little mingling of Protestants with Roman Catholics in such matters. The parochial schools, the orphanages and hospitals, the guilds, sodalities, societies, clubs, camps, are as separate as the Y.M.C.A. from the Knights of Columbus. Protestants do not even give credit to Roman Catholics for the enormous number and the excellence of their schools, hospitals, and orphanages. They regard them merely as a means to an end—propaganda for the ensnaring of souls into the Roman obedience. But, as a matter of fact, the number of conversions to Catholicism in this country is very slight.

Its increase comes almost entirely from immigration.

The social side of the religious life of America would be a study in itself. The machinery and organizations, the suppers and societies, the parish and community houses, the men's clubs and the women's missionary sewing circles, the Sunday-school entertainments, all are calculated to maintain the consciousness of kind and to develop an *esprit de corps*. They are, of course, the remnant of that mediæval solidarity of ecclesiastical and secular life by which the church educated and permeated society for a thousand years. They supplied and perhaps in some places still supply very real needs in a community. But their importance has greatly waned. The extra-ecclesiastical organization of society, the establishment of innumerable non-sectarian fraternal orders, the secularization of education especially, have removed from the churches much of the value of their social activities. Church suppers pall upon the more refined religious groups, strawberry festivals do not pay, the sewing circle no longer meets the need. A missionary can now buy his underwear and his trousers in almost any part of the globe and he is better contented to do so than to have the ladies' aid at the old home church send him misfits. It is easier and less costly to give money outright than to attempt to raise it for church purposes by the old methods. When I was a youth Sunday-school libraries were still in existence. Mr. Carnegie and other agencies have now made that device unnecessary. Sunday-school libraries have virtually disappeared from the earth.

The clergy generally regard these social organizations as a means for the development of loyalty and as feeders of the devotional life of the church on Sundays. It is quite certain that social activities do develop a consciousness of kind, relate people to the parochial organization, and keep up the membership lists. But it often happens that there is no appreciable increase in church attendance through this means.

A church may be highly organized so far as social life is concerned and still have small congregations. The young people enjoy the cakes and such ale as churches nowadays dispense, but they are bored by religious services.

In point of church attendance Protestantism has no effective rules or regulations requiring its members to go to church. Neither has it any attractive forms of worship. It has almost completely lost the idea of worship. There is nothing worth while looking at. The sermon is the main feature of Protestant worship. Often it is excellent. The eloquent divine plays upon the emotions and supplies by the skill of oratory all that is missing in color and movement in the service. He is trained to that end. His ability is the measure of his success. It determines the size of his congregation and the prosperity of his church. If he is a dud, things go down. He must keep up with the times and devise continually new means to interest his group. A difficult business.

90

The great strength of Roman Catholicism, on the other hand, lies in its maintenance of the splendid tradition of worship. Architecturally their churches, having recovered from the bad period of rococo art and the debased Hibernian taste of the last century, are imposing and effective. They have the elements of mystery and devotion. The great altar. The twinkling lights. The scent of incense. The gorgeous vestments. The movement and color. The solemn and stately music of the Mass by some composer of the first rank. The crowds of adoring worshipers. "It beats," as has been suggested, "the devil." The Roman Catholic requirement that every member of the church should attend mass on Sundays under pain of mortal sin, of ultimate expulsion from the communion of the church, from Christian burial, brings out certainly a very large proportion of the membership on Sundays. It is generally conceded in America that Roman Catholics are the only Christians who make church-going a regular business. The sparse congregations in Protestant churches on a rainy Sunday contrast strikingly with the crowded basilicas of the papal obedience.

All the advertising methods, the "go-getter" laymen, the sensational preachers, the advocates of "selling religion," that Protestantism adopts cannot equal the silent and effective system of Rome in the matter of securing church attendance. Congregations of Protestants may boom numerically for a time and sometimes, under favorable circumstances, for a long time. But since they have no principle behind the vogue, when the new voice becomes old or the new sensational method is stale, the numbers fall off and turn to something more novel.

VI

America has been called a Christian country. Even after one has admitted that there are less than forty-five per cent. of the nation enrolled in any religious denomination and that in the list must be counted all the Jews as well as an enormous number of religions that can scarcely be called Christian, it is probably true that America is a Christian country. For the leading elements here, though they may not be active church members or exemplify certain of the recognized Christian qualities, still hold in respect the ideals of Christianity. They are potentially Christian. Moreover, it cannot be denied that at least the openly professed standards and moral ideals hold to the tradition of historic Christianity. If men differ vastly in regard to their duty towards God, they at least agree in a general way on their duty towards their neighbor. The nation will respond with incredible generosity to any valid charity. Humanitarianism is in the air. Never in the world's history have the rich men of any nation initiated or sustained such vast enterprises of public charity.

But while there are great works for the benefit of our fellow men, it remains true that the sums given for churches and their distinctive enterprises do not equal the amounts contributed to general educational and humanitarian enterprises. To be sure, the expense of maintenance of the variety of sects is enormous in the aggregate and there are instances of individual gifts to missions and buildings of large proportions. But the churches for the most part are sustained by the numerous contributions in small amounts extracted from the faithful by the urgent efforts of their pastors. The Episcopal Church, for example, contains a very large number of multimillionaires, but it is a constant complaint on the part of the clergy that while rich men give generously to colleges that have nothing to do with the church and even to institutions of other denominations, as well as to general public charities, they give very small sums indeed for the work of Episcopalian missions, Episcopalian colleges, and other Episcopalian enterprises. This is equally true of the other religious bodies with a few notable exceptions among the Methodists and Baptists. It is an evidence that the givers feel little confidence in sectarian ideals. Perhaps they doubt the permanence of their own churches. In the richest country in the world the churches are continually howling for money to keep going. The largest part of the energy is consumed in efforts to raise funds. The Protestant churches are often in debt and behind in their budget. They are forced to have "campaigns" to keep afloat.

In point of individual conduct it would probably make little difference in the national morality if all the churches in the country were closed to-morrow. Morality is a matter of race inheritance, of custom and of law. The intrusion of the churches into the making of laws has generally resulted in producing worse rather than better conditions. The prisons are full of criminals who have been brought up by God-fearing parents, have attended Sunday-school or parochial schools, and in their youth went to church. It appears that those religions that are the most strict in the care of their young and insist upon

95

careful religious education also contribute the largest numbers to our penal institutions. In thirty years' experience I have found just as many good and honest people who are outside the churches, atheists and agnostics, as I have found inside. And there are plenty of cranks, crooks, criminals, and liars who are active in churches and even very pious in outward appearance on the church rolls. Everybody who has served on a Grand Jury knows that ninety per cent. of the cases considered and true bills drawn are of foreign-born people who have invariably had in their youth a thorough religious training.

But it would solve many of the problems of religion and be in the interest of economy and the public good if religion were under state control in America. Religious education would then be reasonably uniform. Religion would be sustained and regulated. The jarring wars of sects would cease. Religion would become respectable. There can be no doubt that the present ef-

forts of the churches to control the state will result, as it always has resulted historically, in
the state controlling the churches. That day is
far off, but it is coming.

THE BREAK-UP OF PROTESTANTISM

INSTITUTIONS die hard. Especially religious institutions. They take a long time about it. Generations and centuries. The nostalgia of religious habits. The endowments and vested interests. Paganism and the mysteries lingered long in the Empire even after Constantine. It is doubtful if they ever did die entirely. Syncretism kept them alive even in the church itself. Perhaps nothing really dies. Religious values at least assert the prerogative of immortality. They modify and affect the movements that absorb them.

But Protestantism *as an organized religious force* is moribund and shows signs of rapid disintegration.

This does not mean that the millions of Methodists, Baptists, Congregationalists, Presbyterians, and the two hundred other Protestant sects will come cringing and bowing down to the coped and mitred hierarchy, kissing the amethyst rings of bishops and cardinals, repentant prodigals begging for instruction and reception. Not at all. We are still too near the ages of persecution, the rack and thumbscrew, the Inquisition, Foxe's "Book of Martyrs," "Westward Ho!" and the religious wars to feel confidence in that direction. Anti-Roman prejudice is in the blood. A race inheritance. Protestantism will still protest.

Moreover the educated, the critically intellectual multitudes,—a rapidly increasing number,—show no disposition to submit to religious autocracy. If they have conceived of the Bible as a broken reed or a quagmire, there is no reason to think that they will turn to ecclesiastics swathed in the traditions of dead centuries for guidance to the high places of eternity. They share with the rabble a fixed antipathy to the graded hierarchy, the elaborate ceremonies, plaster images, meretricious decoration of churches, superstitions and fetishism, local Heavens and literal Hells, meticulous doctrines

99

and obsolete philosophies, celibacy and monachism, the assumption of a superior and esoteric knowledge, the tendency to political domination, the assertion of a defined and certain finality in the possession of truth.

A disintegrated Protestantism will no more return to Rome than the troubled democracy of the day will return to the frozen archaism of the feudal system. If Protestanism as an organized religious force is dying in the twentieth century, by the same tokens of broken authority Rome died in the sixteenth.

Autocratic authority in religion is everywhere giving ground.

I

The famous historian, Bishop Stubbs of Oxford, who married his cook, used to advise his students to avoid generalization and idealization. It is good advice for the incipient historian. The Bishop's books are dull reading, but they are eminently sound. It is temerarious to draw very definite conclusions about wide popular movements, and above all to make prophecies. But many able observers of the present condition of the religious world are persuaded that we are in the midst of a religious revolution. There is reason to believe that the historians of a hundred years from now will pronounce the present decade the crest of a movement more significant and portentous than the Reformation itself.

The Reformation, considered as a religious revolution, took its rise in the social and political consequences of the discoveries of the fifteenth century, the fall of Constantinople, the Renaissance, the rise of nations, the growth of commerce. The break from Rome in the sixteenth century was its crisis. For two centuries the religious settlements of that period stood secure. But about a hundred years ago, before the middle of the nineteenth century, new movements were set afoot which were destined to bring about a still greater crisis. With this crisis we are now face to face. As the authority of Rome was shattered in those nations which followed the trend of thought at the Reformation, so the Reformation settlements now find their authority shattered by the logical consequences of the position they then took.

If Rome appears to be little affected by the movements of the day, that is because the genius of Rome has never been expressed in intellectual leadership, but, by settled policy and highly developed organization, in deliberate conservatism. She has assimilated movements, not started them. Ministering as she does to the masses of uneducated and simple people, such a position is both reasonable and necessary. For there is nothing so unsettling to the stability of religious authority, and hence to morals, as a new idea. Rome kept on the Index Expurgatorius until 1829 every book that said the world was round. The theologians all knew better, but why disturb the masses? Are not the stars the eyes of

the angels looking down from Heaven? And what difference does it make to the man with the hoe if they are not? Let girls in Spanish convents continue thus to regard the stars—and be good.

But Protestantism, which was the progressive party of the Catholic Church in the sixteenth century, with a sense of the unity of all truth and a passionate and even stupid literalism, must go on to complete the programme it then began. Having broken fearlessly with any authority that conflicted with its conscientious conception of truth, it is logically forced to continue the process. It must complete its work. No antique hocus-pocus, no prescriptive documentation, no hallowed tradition, may hold it back from the truth and freedom. Hitching its wagon to Betelgeuse, of which it knows the size and chemical constituents, Protestantism now determines to make a clean sweep of all the remnants of tyranny and obscurantism that have still bound it back from freedom. It proposes

103

a twentieth-century revolution. At least it finds itself in the midst of one.

And it is greatly to be wished that, in the process of housecleaning, Protestantism shall sweep out into the dust-heap of time its own superstitions and hypocrisies, its petty partisanships and false loyalties, its narrow nationalisms and racial peculiarities, its sentimental cant, its vapid prayer meetings, its redundant and verbose liturgies, its stodgy services, its preposterous confessions of faith, its bigotry and prejudices, its padded and fictitious martyrologies, its smug self-satisfactions, its holier-than-thou pose, its lay popes, its fond and fanatical trust in secular legislation, its bitter intolerance, its suspicious and terrible emotionalisms, its assumption that mere negation constitutes salvation, and the thousand and one other Pecksniffian attributes that in its name have so often brought all religion into contempt among sensible people. Let the good work be thoroughly done this time, and not stopped by any premature armistice.

104

II

That the revolution is well under way cannot be doubted. It had become apparent as early as the middle of the last century that the foundations upon which Protestantism rested—the Bible and the various Reformation settlements —were insecure. Dr. Ewer, in his "Failure of Protestantism," pointed out the fallacy that the Bible, the books of which were selected by the authority of the church, could properly supplant that authority. Logically the Bible was an instrument, not a foundation for the church. There was a church, with its creed, sacraments, and ministry, before the books of the New Testament were written, and centuries before the canon of Scripture was determined. Chillingworth's dictum, "The Bible and the Bible only is the religion of Protestants," became an illogical absurdity. Ewer followed the Oxford Tractarians and the Anglican tradition.

But it remained for the German higher critics to reduce the stronghold of a superstitious reverence for the printed word. Protestantism, which had substituted a printed book for a living Pope, was aghast. But its passion for truth has compelled it to admit the facts. Although the clamor of the war between the Fundamentalists and so-called Modernists still continues, it is evident to every scholarly observer that Fundamentalism is a lost cause.

As the cracks in the foundation appeared and their significance began to be grasped, Protestant enthusiasm weakened. The first evidence of this was in Sunday-school attendance. Up to the eighties the statistical curve had shown a steady increase. In the late eighties it began steadily to decline. It has fallen rapidly ever since. The latest report indicates that there are now over twenty-seven millions of American children, nominally Protestant, not enrolled in any Sunday-school. And quite reasonably. The Protestant Sunday-school has no systematized religion to

106

teach. With the old Reformation catechisms and
confessions gone increasingly out of use, and
nothing but the Bible left as a book of instruction, the teachers—generally untrained and in-
competent as teachers of anything—had depended for interest upon making little children
learn the list of the kings of Israel and Judah,
the names of the bugs on the Plain of Esdraelon,
who was Moses' uncle, how long was the bed
of Og, the king of Bashan, and the missionary
journeys of the Apostle Paul. Some elaborate
books, like "The Christian Nurture Series," were
indeed devised to meet the condition, but as
these insisted on treating infants as though they
were small philosophers, they were ineffective.
The Sunday-school, now called the church-school,
has become the despair or the joke of the Protestant ministry almost everywhere. The attendance
of both teachers and pupils is generally small
and irregular. Few ministers are able to keep
up any system of devotion, spiritual value, or
inspiration among the young. Nor has the week-

day school of religion yet met the case. Parents, persuaded that the Bible as a document of scientific and historical facts is under fire, are no longer insistent upon sending their already weary children to such dull exercises.

The Roman Catholics, on the other hand, with daily religious instruction in their schools, using the clear-cut, definite, and positive teaching of the Baltimore catechism, with its system of doctrine, discipline, and worship, with daily attendance at mass, continued the authoritative teaching in which the church and not the Bible was the final court of appeal. The result is patent. Ask any Roman Catholic child a fundamental question about his religion and you get a categorical answer. You may not agree with the answer, but it is an answer. Ask, on the other hand, almost any Protestant child a similar question—well, just try it and see for yourself. Our Protestant grandparents had at least some definite religion as children. The present generation has none.

Combined with the critical attitude of the age is the general laxity which always comes with financial success. "When the Puritans made their fortunes," said James Russell Lowell, "they lost their religion." Add the dazzling and wonderful strides of scientific discovery, the golf course, the automobile, and finally the radio, with comfortable sermons by famous preachers on Sunday for those disposed to listen, and you have some at least of the chief causes of a decline in church attendance. Life is speeded up. People are tired on Sunday. The fashion of going to church is falling off.

III

For the past twenty years desperate efforts have been made by Protestant leaders to keep up the failing enthusiasm for church organization. All kinds of leagues and conferences, sometimes with excellent, if temporary, results, were started. The Men and Religion Forward Move-

109

ment, the Men's Missionary Movement, Young People's Movements, revivals of all kinds, swept the country. Finally Billy Sunday—a genius for the stirring of religious emotionalism—galvanized for his brief day the churches into a semblance of vitality. Every adult reader will remember these struggles to sustain the slipping structure. It was one hope, not so fully recognized during the war, that the Y.M.C.A. would perhaps take over the whole work of the Protestant churches and rehabilitate it. But, in spite of the millions of dollars in hand, it became evident that the men in the ranks did not feel that the combination of vaudeville and sermon which the "Y" proposed to substitute for religion would do. The plan, if it was ever formulated, was given up.

Experts in the guise of secretaries were called in. After the war great sums of money were raised, or promised, in all the divisions of the Protestant world. Great missionary enterprises were planned. It was assumed that if interest in foreign missions could be aroused the interest in the old home church would be sustained. But within five years the churches were as much in debt as ever. The Inter-Church Federation, with very able men in its offices, studied the problem, and is even yet endeavoring to uphold the tottering steeples. Dr. Cadman preaches eloquently over the radio from the Bedford branch of the Brooklyn Y.M.C.A. on Sunday afternoons with the same object, in a spirit of broad tolerance—one of the best things that Protestantism can do to foster liberal piety.

But the thing that has kept Protestantism alive as an organized force during recent years has undoubtedly been the Prohibition movement. For years the temperance societies, the W.C.T.U., and the Anti-Saloon League have kept total abstinence and the desire for legislative action against the Demon Rum as a rallying point for the organized activity of the Protestant churches. The recent revelations before the Senate investigating committee have shown the enormous sums of money collected by these agencies from the churches for use in this campaign. Billy Sunday always made it a chief article in his creed. ("Hell has frozen over," he declared when the Eighteenth Amendment was passed.) Other skilled and highly paid workers were employed to carry on. Methods not always scrupulous, but justified in the eyes of enthusiastic "dry" Protestants on the ground that the end justified the means,—a theory that Protestants formerly strongly condemned as Jesuit practice,—were used in every state in the Union to ensure the success of this crusade. For years Prohibition formed the chief subject of Protestant preaching. It is probably no exaggeration to say that nearly every pastor of certain denominations either made it the theme of his Sunday sermon or at least referred to it strongly in his discourse, making it practically a *sine qua non* in religion.

It does not seem to have occurred to many that the Bible as an authoritative book in reality suffered more from the emphasis upon Prohibition than it had suffered from all the critical literature ever written by German or other critics. The critics had merely shown up the facts of historicity. They had allowed the moral and spiritual values to stand on their own intrinsic merits. But in advocating Prohibition the Protestant clergy were compelled to criticize the very morality of the Gospel. The marriage at Cana, where Jesus turned the water into wine, when men had "well drunk," became reprehensible. The advice to Timothy "to use a little wine" was given in ignorance. The very matter of the sacrament of the Lord's Supper was regarded as intrinsically evil. Unfermented grape juice was generally substituted. The Pauline discourses about the provocative character of negative legislation were always passed over. It was even proposed to get out an edition of the Bible with all the passages that referred to wine deleted. In short, the Bible in the house of its friends became a dangerous book. Many parts of it could

113

not possibly be read in Protestant churches. They would contradict the sermon.

But now that the methods by which Prohibition was put over have been exposed,—its failure to freeze up Hell everywhere becoming apparent, the evils of it constantly more pressing,—reaction has set in. Division on the subject even in the ranks of the pastors will follow. Already the Lutherans have come out strongly against it. Episcopalians in increasing numbers refuse to praise its works. Conventions, synods, and assemblies are less unanimous in voting resolutions supporting the law. Prohibition as a religious rallying point will fail. In reality it is not a religious issue. Temperance, yes; but not Prohibition.

IV

Fissiparism is the evil genius of Protestantism. Indeed the theory of private judgment suggests that its ultimate and logical trend is to-

114

ward sheer individualism. Certain it is that the efforts which have been made to draw the Protestant sects together, to economize expense, to prevent duplication of labor, to establish some sort of comity, to realize any degree of unity in organization,—such as the Edinburgh Conference, the Inter-Church Federation, the World Conference on Faith and Order,—have made no real progress in the elimination of the sectarian spirit. On the contrary. It is certain that at the present time there is less hope of church unity than there was twenty years ago. Some leaders even feel that division is an advantage and makes for progress in religious thought. Some look upon sectarianism as one would look upon the distinctions of family life. The nostalgia of accustomed habits holds them. They feel a suspicion of other forms of devotion.

The proposal to hold a World Conference on Faith and Order, originating in Anglican circles, lent some hope for a time that spiritual unity, if not corporate unity, could be attained. The commissions and secretariats responsible for this undertaking, however, have put off the actual conference from year to year on the plea that premature corporate unity would have worse results than the present condition. They have urged a general study of the causes of separation in small local conferences, questions of sacraments and episcopacy, and creeds and episcopacy, and the validity of orders and episcopacy, and liturgies and episcopacy, and church polity and episcopacy, and episcopacy, until the idea has gone abroad that the astute Anglican bishops who are behind the movement are in reality merely carrying on a campaign of education of the non-conformist ministry in the hope of persuading Protestantism to make a little pilgrimage to Canterbury or to go a few parasangs on the road to Rome. Bishops, whether Anglican, Oriental, or Roman, are monarchs who desire not to abdicate.

There is, then, no hope of unity among Protestants. That idea must be quite definitely laid

116

aside. The cutthroat methods of rivalry, of over-churching, will continue. Every little group in every new community, obsessed by some racial or social inferiority complex, will insist upon having an ecclesiastical background upon which to display itself. Our small towns will continue to be dotted with buildings called churches, more suitable for garages than for teocallis, without dignity, without beauty either inside or out, their few members struggling to keep the sheriff from closing the doors on account of the unpaid coal bill, and starving the very soul out of the poor wretch of a pastor who presides in the pulpit on Sundays. The only persons benefited by the system are the secretaries, bishops, presiding elders, arch-deacons, missionary boards, and other paid remote functionaries who thrive on division and justify their salaries by the published records of new enterprises.

The divisions that exist even inside the same denomination are equally deep. Anglicanism itself, which for many years looked upon itself

117

as the *via media,* a possible rallying point for both Catholic and Protestant, is becoming little less than a line of cleavage. Two parties, Catholic and Protestant, threaten to tear the communion asunder. Among the sects the Fundamentalists and Modernists have so divided the groups that it is not too much to say that scarcely any two churches of the same denomination teach the same religion. And the rivalry that exists between two churches of different denominations is as naught compared with the rivalry that exists between two churches of the same denomination in the same town. At bottom there is the economic factor. A pastor cannot afford to let one sheep escape. It will affect the budget. The actual beliefs of a man in the pew become matters of comparative indifference—so long as he remains in the pew. If he goes to another church, he is a heretic.

It is not an evidence of disintegration or revolution that there are now over fifty-eight millions of Americans, nominally Protestant, not enrolled as members of any church, or that only one third of those so enrolled attend churches with any regularity or contribute to the support of churches. Careful surveys show this to be the case. But conditions were worse a hundred years ago. The percentage of those attending churches, where it was not compulsory, in colonial days was smaller. That would not mean that the organization is necessarily breaking up. Religion comes in waves. It is emotional. Given a great cause or a spiritual access, the churches might be filled to-morrow. Even Roman Catholics have their "paschal lambs," those who come only for their Easter duties. A revival of religious enthusiasm might sweep the country any day.

But it is significant of a decided change that in very many churches the old type of devotion, the solemnity of religious worship, the serious and long sermon, have passed away. The pastors, even when fine orators, men of ability and magnetic force and learning, are put to it more

119

and more to fill their auditoriums. There is a general tendency to resort to popular lectures, moving pictures, Rotarian methods, church suppers, wild advertising, a studied display of the "glad hand," follow-up letters, a paid official to detect the arrival of any newcomer to town and sign him up, programs of sensational sermon courses, cartoonists, whistlers, comedians, enormous signs on the church porch, dwarfs, Indians, Negro Jubilee singers, freaks of all sorts, free ginger ale, services conducted exclusively by children, and a thousand other Chautauqua devices, in the hope of drawing a crowd—a crowd that pays nothing.

The fact is that the old feeling of an obligation to attend service on the part of the laity has almost vanished from the earth. The members of churches feel no obligation whatever. They go or stay away as they like. They also pay what they like. The average Protestant church is like a club in which they are no conditions of membership, no dues, no responsibilities. It

120

has become a purely voluntary association of individuals who determine for themselves the articles of their belief, and whose motive for church attendance is not much higher in many instances than their motive for attending a theater, a popular lecture, a concert, or a motion picture. Recognition of authority or religious obligation has almost disappeared. Pressure of any sort to compel such recognition would instantly be resented and usually result in withdrawal from the church.

Under these circumstances what likelihood is there that organization can long continue to exist?

V

But the actual force that is disrupting Protestantism is the force of money. As in all revolutionary movements, the economic factor is the final cause. Almost any organization can withstand attacks from without and weakness within

so long as the purse strings are in the hands of
the leaders. The natural leaders of the Protestant
churches are the ministers. But the money of
most of these churches is controlled by laymen.
In those churches where the controlling laymen
are quasi-ecclesiastics—deacons, elders, men of
prayer—conditions are less bad than in those
where the laymen have no spiritual status. But
generally speaking the control of the finances is
in the wrong hands. If the ministers who do the
preaching and thereby raise the money also had
the spending of it, the organizations would hold
out long against time and storm.

This is an idea very foreign, however, to the
Protestant mind. Most Protestants, speaking re-
ligiously, regard the idea of handling filthy
lucre as something improper for a spiritual man.
They think of the saying in the Book of Acts
about the serving of tables, but forget that other
passage about laying the money derived from
the sale of their lands at the apostles' feet. Historically it is clear that down to the time of the

122

Reformation the clergy always controlled the affairs of the church. And the church grew rich —some say too rich. In the Roman Church it is the clergy who handle the money yet, and there is no business in the world so well handled.

Now the minister is responsible for the financial success of every church. Even if he happens to be backed by some millionaire, he has attracted the millionaire. If money does not come in as the result of his preaching and work, he is a failure. But it is the lay board, the vestry, the trustees, who take the money he secures, determine his salary, and pay the bills of the church. They themselves give usually but a small portion of the amount raised. The minister has a life-and-death stake in the matter. The laymen have none.

If follows that the minister, who may be presumed to have a professional knowledge of the needs of his church, of the kind of building that should be erected, of the type of music to be hired, of all the details of the enterprise, is not

123

the real director of the affairs of the church, but merely an employee of a lay group. It is an anomalous position. He is the nominal head of a business with none of the authority of the head. There are exceptions, of course, but the scene in the first act of Mr. Golden's production, "Thank You," is not in the least exaggerated.

The men on the lay boards are either men of such large affairs that the business of a church is too petty for their consideration—it has become increasingly difficult to get meetings of such men, as every director of a big business knows—or they are apt to be men of petty minds and small experience, without faith and without vision. Able and devoted men in such offices are becoming rare, and are confined mostly to the large cities. Not infrequently these church officials are very difficult for the average minister, unused to dealing with people under the rough conditions of the business world. Since they hold the purse strings, he is powerless.

The consequences of this method of administration, except in the case of pastors of unusual genius and powerful personality, can be clearly defined. Without knowledge, without vision, without faith, with no higher motive than economy and the fear of venture, many lay boards erect mean, cheap structures on obscure, cheap sites. Their chief concern is to scale down the architect's dream and to save money. The glory of God and the splendor of worship seldom enter their heads. Every pastor who has built a church, and every architect, knows the infinite ineptitude of these men. It is not so much their fault, however, as the fault of the system which places them in a position they are unfitted to occupy. And it is this same system which, making the real head of church affairs not the pastor but an irresponsible lay board, puts so much of the church work in many places into the hands of the "little mousy men who are religious," to the annoyance and despair of the nominal leader, who is powerless to direct affairs because he is a mere hired man.

When Dr. Herbert Hensley Henson, now Bishop of Durham, visited this country he said that the great weakness of the Protestant churches both in Canada and in the United States was the dependence of the ministers on the good-will of the people. He was right. And it is the failure of the clergy to control and direct the finances of their churches that makes them thus dependent. Barring the wild self-appointed preachers of the hills, the fanatics, the cranks, and the sentimental uplifters, the ordained and licensed Protestant ministers of the American towns and villages will compare favorably with any group of business or professional men. Generally better educated than the average of the congregations to whom they preach, better read, more open-minded, more ready to try new methods and to receive new ideas, certainly as competent to direct and control the finances of their churches as the clergy of the Church of Rome, they find themselves merely hirelings of

126

groups they are compelled to please and whom they dare not stimulate or rebuke.

The professional success of the Protestant minister depends upon his ability to raise money. That does not mean that he need even mention the subject. It means that he must have the qualities of leadership, of organization, of spiritual power, of eloquence or magnetism, in sufficient degree to cause people to give. The church must be kept out of debt, his own salary must be raised, the enormous demands of the bishops, boards, and secretaries in the general offices must be satisfied; otherwise the minister is a failure. It all depends upon him, yet the minister is considered too holy to be interested in who gives or what is given, to be too spiritual to attend to the business affairs of his church, too other-worldly to know enough to handle the finances of his parish.

It is a tribute to the ability of the Protestant ministry that they have managed so well with

127

so impossible a system. But it accounts for the constant changes in the pastorate, the miserable salaries paid to ministers, and the decay of church organization. For the prayer of the average layman for his pastor seems to be, "O Lord, you keep him humble, and we'll keep him poor."

VI

Protestantism, then, is undergoing a revolution. The foundation of authority upon which it was built has certainly shifted, if not broken. Considered as an organization, or as organizations, the Protestant churches might weather that storm, just as the Roman Church has held together under centuries of criticism, were it not for the fact that the real leadership in Protestant organization is not in the hands of professional leaders, but in the hands of laymen. Such men, not having time, training, or a vital stake in the cause of religion, confused by external interests and doubts regarding the foundations of their

128

churches, cannot rescue the sinking vessel. Protestantism is disintegrating and is doomed. It may outlast your life and mine, but ultimately America will see it no more.

It is my conviction that the sooner Protestantism disappears from American life the better. Its narrow sectarian spirit, fostering division, incapable of a large synthesis of values, of unity, unfits it to represent our national religious life. Its differences of polity and doctrine, of forms and customs, do not justify the expense of its duplication of effort and upkeep. It does not answer to the deep needs of human nature. As a moral guide it is superficial, depending on the exterior force of state legislation to effect the redemption of the race. As a mystical experience it is sentimental, without intelligence, and with narrow vision. As a teaching force it is vague, negative, and uncertain. As an organization it is illogical and chaotic.

Considered in relation to the idea of worship, Protestantism is particularly lacking. It began by eliminating the element of beauty from its meeting-houses, and it has never succeeded in bringing it back. At the best its services are coldly dignified. At the worst they are slovenly and drab. Without color. Without movement. But beauty is an attribute of God and should be expressed in worship. There is no wonder that men prefer the ceremonies of the lodge, with the vestments, lights, moving acolytes, and swinging incense, to the undecorated dullness of their Sunday worship.

The strength of Protestantism has been in preaching. But in these days of general culture, of the radio and the newspaper, even those to whom the sermon is still something of a saving ordinance find it less necessary to attend church for the purpose of hearing one. Why go to the trouble of dressing for the church parade when you can sit at home and hear a preacher of the first rank instead of the third-rate man who occupies the pulpit in the old home town? And preaching at its best does not reach down into

130

the depths of the individual life sufficiently to have great moral value. It is too general. The average Protestant pastor is much like a physician who should find himself limited in practice to the giving of one or two lectures a week on the general subject of hygiene in the ward of a hospital. Compared with the individual relationship of the pastor to the sinner in the Catholic confessional, Protestantism with all its preaching is merely on the outside of life.

Moreover, there are many subjects upon which the Protestant preacher for various reasons can scarcely touch. Remember that above all things he must please his audience. Otherwise they will not come again, they will not support him, they will persuade his board, his trustees, his vestry, to get rid of him. The average pastor is paid less than a cook, less than a chauffeur, less than an unskilled laborer. If he gets out of a job, it is by no means easy for him to obtain another readily. The organizations of Protestant churches feel no obligation to provide him with a place. Unless he is a dominant personality with considerable gifts of leadership he must above all things avoid offense. If he has been long in the ministry and has given hostages to fortune, it is a tragedy for him to lose even the miserable pittance he receives. It is to the honor of the men in the profession that so many of them risk unpopularity and even livelihood by having the courage of their convictions.

Protestantism has never developed a moral theology. Consider, for instance, its dealing with the vital subject of sex. This vast and most important aspect of human life is seldom dealt with in any thorough fashion in Protestant teaching. If handled at all, it is touched upon very gingerly. Unsuitable for the subject of pulpit oratory, it has become the Great Taboo of the Protestant world. Protestantism can make no provision for the instruction of adolescent youth on this profound matter. It leaves youth to its own guidance, the guidance of ill-instructed parents, or such information as it may chance to pick up from whatever sources. And the consequences of this failure in religious instruction are abundantly apparent.

The old disciplinary systems by which the lay members of Protestant churches were bound to profess certain beliefs, to maintain certain rules of conduct, and to sustain certain obligations to the church on pain of loss of membership, have become as obsolete as the old formulas, the confessions of faith. Where they still remain on the books they are practically dead letters. The decline in the numbers of the church membership, the desperate need of money, the intense rivalry of sectarianism, combined with the liberal spirit of the age, have swept them into the discard. Most churches will do anything for anybody—receive anybody, marry anybody, bury anybody. They hawk their sacred wares about the streets. They cry aloud for people to fill their large and empty buildings. They offer inducements for those connected with other churches to leave their accustomed pastures and try new ones. The organizations are without confidence and without dignity. They are breaking up.

VII

But far more important than any study of these defects and conditions, now for a generation known and recognized, is the consideration of what will take the place of this outworn and dying system. What will follow the break-up of Protestantism?

Some have felt with Chesterton that Rome will be the residuary legatee, the Pope the universal landlord. They point to what Rome has to offer. In convenience. In uniformity. In artistic forms of worship. In architectural splendor. Rome is the least expensive church to belong to in all Christendom. Its system of finance, managed by the clerical order, is effective. Its elaborate and settled organization, its united front and vast size, give it weight politically and socially. Its lay members are not bothered with

134

the necessity of thinking out religious problems for themselves. The complexity and variety of its cults and doctrines enable one to make choice of those features of Christianity that suit one's temperament and mood. It is tolerant enough unless you venture to question too publicly. Perhaps for a time Roman Catholicism may become the fashion.

But, as I said at the beginning, the values of religious institutions never die. The undying values of Protestantism are the passionate assertion of liberty and truth. Protestantism shook off Rome once. It will never revert in any permanent and final way to the acceptance of religious authority. It is, in the present revolution, shaking off the remnants of such authority. The new generation will begin to think where such organization as Protestantism still supports leaves off, to assume the death of that for which it still argues.

Perhaps in dying as an organized force Protestantism will in reality save itself. The church after all is a means to an end, not an end in itself. When the author of the Apocalypse saw the heavenly vision, he saw no temple there. The church, in a sense, exists merely to do away with the need of its existence. But what new form the spirit of religion in the coming age may take, who can say?

Is it not reasonable to hope that, leaving the outworn dogmatisms and methods of the past, the children of the new age will construct out of those values which have been the real sources of inspiration and of power, both for Catholic and Protestant, a church that will meet the needs of the day and generation, combining with the old the new wisdom of the present era, raising mankind to a higher plane of spiritual experience, a more vivid realization of eternal life?

"Every scribe which is instructed unto the kingdom of heaven is like unto a man that is an householder, which bringeth forth out of his treasure things new and old."

136

THE CHIMÆRA OF CHURCH UNITY

I

"IF there were only one church in the world," President Dwight of Yale used to say, "I should feel that I had a call from God to go out and start another one."

In every department of human knowledge except religion the attainment of truth has now for a long time been regarded as progressive. In religion it was and is yet conceived as something long since fully revealed, fixed and final. There could be no progress. Newman, indeed, advanced the theory of development, but this was merely the explicit formulation of what had already been known implicitly.

It is only in comparatively recent times that intellectual religious men have come to think of religious knowledge as being in the same cate-

gory with all other knowledge, a matter of
progress. How far they so regard it, is still uncertain. But, since division is a necessity of
progress, they feel suspicious of the movement
for a united and highly organized church. Such
a church would inhibit progress, limit freedom
of thought, hinder investigation. That is always
the tendency of intrenched and settled authority,
both in church and state. Division, even organized division, insures greater freedom. You can
turn the rascals out—or leave them.

With its hundreds of millions of followers it
is surprising that there is as much unanimity of
opinion in Christianity as there is. There are
racial divisions and cultural differences, college
presidents and savages, statesmen and jailbirds,
intellectuals and masses of unwashed peasants,
all over the green world, and all alike claim a
share in the benefits of religion as their most
precious heritage. To each individual his religion is what it is irrespective of what others
may have. There are similarities, but there are

138

also differences. Probably no two people have quite the same ideas on the subject.

The problem is further complicated by the fact that religion is not merely an intellectual attainment. It is also a matter of the heart, the feelings, the will. Probably chiefly that. Over and above exterior and formal unity there is the question of spiritual unity, of brotherhood, the love of man as well as the love of God. Within the ranks of the same organizations envy, hatred, and malice, and all uncharitableness may destroy the spirit of unity which is essential to the idea. A rift in feeling is more apt to create schism than any intellectual differences. While good men who disagree can manage to keep together, a parochial quarrel often starts a new church. The village choir, the lay popes, male and female, clerical professional jealousy, are decisive factors in Protestant churches, often more potent than theological debate. Browning's "Soliloquy in a Spanish Cloister" illustrates the possibility among Catholics.

Gr-r-r—there go, my heart's abhorrence!
  Water your damned flower-pots, do!
If hate killed men, Brother Lawrence,
  God's blood, would not mine kill you?
What? your myrtle-bush wants trimming?
  Oh, that rose has prior claims—
Needs its leaden vase filled brimming?
  Hell dry you up with its flames!

Not this side of Paradise therefore—when the
redeemed shall have attained to Ultimate Truth
and walk in the white robes of irreversible charity—is church unity, corporate and spiritual, a
possibility. Like communism its programme implies a condition where men are as the angels of
God. It is a Counsel of Perfection. How far are
we moving in its direction?

II

Cardinal Newman, after his conversion, felt
that truth was to be found not in the *Via Media*
but in extremes. Certainly the extreme positions
in the matter of religion are more readily stated
and easier to grasp.

140

On the one hand there is the Roman Catholic position. This is that unity consists in being in communion with the Bishop of Rome, commonly called the Pope—the title of all bishops in ancient times, from *pater*, "father." In the Roman Catholic Church the Bishop of Rome is the supreme authority. He is the Vicar of Christ. When he speaks *ex cathedra*, that is, as head of the church, his decisions are final and indisputable. If it happens that you do not agree with what he says on matters of faith and morals, you must either change your belief, get out, or be put out. The applies quite as much to the laity as to the clergy.

It is true that there is some difficulty in determining when the pope speaks *ex cathedra* as distinguished from his opinions as an individual. For example, the decrees of Pius IX on the doctrines of the Immaculate Conception of the Blessed Virgin Mary and Papal Infallibility are universally regarded as *ex cathedra* utterances. But I am told by certain pundits that the bull of

141

Leo XIII declaring Anglican orders invalid is not *ex cathedra*, but merely the opinion of one pope as a theologian. And it is well known that the very definite directions of the late Pius X on church music are utterly disregarded by large numbers of Roman Catholic clergy, presumably on the ground that they are not *ex cathedra*.

Theoretically, however, the pope is the supreme court and ultimate sole authority in the Roman Catholic Church. He is the voice of tradition, the interpreter of conciliar decrees, the expounder of dogma, the judge in all disputes. To be sure, he operates through an elaborate system of delegated authority, the College of Cardinals, the various courts, such as the Rota, the Congregation of Sacred Rites, the Propaganda, a diplomatic corps, legates (*legati nati et a latere*), apostolic delegates, patriarchs, archbishops, bishops, and priests. And decisions on most matters have long ago been made and are readily available. Only great and very important matters come before the pope himself, but he

142

appoints the officials and can reverse their decisions, as history shows, when he will. *Roma locuta est, causa finita est,* was a mediæval proverb which still holds.

You will notice in this connection that one never sees nowadays in public prints, books, magazines or elsewhere, any speculative articles on fundamental subjects written by Roman Catholic clergymen. This is not because Roman Catholic clergymen do not write well. It is because it would be extremely temerarious for them to express themselves publicly on religious topics except in the way of panegyric or apologetic. For practically everything in that religion has been settled, and the cases of such men as the Jesuit Tyrrell and the Abbé Loisy, excommunicated a generation ago for venturing to say what Protestant scholars everywhere accept in regard to Holy Scripture, give the most venturesome reason to pause.

The Roman Catholic system has many practical advantages. It provides a living voice for

143

all matters of dispute in doctrine and morals. As an authoritative system it is easily understood, simple, convenient, and effective. In a sense it is the religion of an individual. But that individual is the Pope, who theoretically merely pronounces the decrees of the universal church. For people of simple minds, for those who do not like speculative thought, for those who want problems in religion settled promptly and definitely, the value of Roman Catholicism cannot be estimated.

Moreover, the uniformity of the Roman Catholic Church, its almost universal presence, the dignity and variety of its services, the extent and effectiveness of its humanitarian institutions, the thoroughness of its organization add enormously to the attraction it offers to the masses of mankind. Its ideals of sanctity, of self-sacrifice, are unexcelled. Its missionary enterprises are vast and effective. Its history is imposing. It is by far the largest of Christian sects.

At the other extreme stands Protestantism.

144

But in dealing with Protestantism a distinction must be made. There are two types of Protestantism. There is popular Protestantism and intellectual Protestantism. The recent American names for them are Fundamentalist and Modernist. The historical and Fundamentalist Protestantism is quite as definitely authoritative as the Roman Catholic Church. It bases its authority, however, not in a living man but in a book, the Bible. The Bible, together with the rules and regulations made by Protestant assemblies, conventions, synods, and councils, from the Reformation period on, are the guiding rules of its faith and conduct. During its earlier period, often allied with the state, Protestantism, at least certain sects of it, maintained a severe discipline both of the laity and of the clergy. Of late years, since its dissociation from state control nearly everywhere, it has been able only to discipline its clergy. The laity do about as they please.

Unfortunately for Protestantism of the historical type, the Bible is subject to a variety of interpretations. In consequence there never was a united Protestantism. There were as many sects as there were interpretations. Whenever there arose a religious leader who felt the importance of some special emphasis on some particular aspect of the Bible, he formed a new sect. And in modern times the higher criticism of the Bible, both Old and New Testaments, has resulted in the division of most of the sects still further. This critical attitude towards the basis of Protestant authority has, in fact, resulted in the creation of a new type of Protestantism, the Modernist or intellectual Protestantism of to-day.

Intellectual Protestantism has something to say for itself. Practically rejecting all prescriptive authority in religion, it places the whole matter of religious knowledge on a par with all other knowledge, historical and scientific. It accepts Scripture as it accepts any other writing, on its intrinsic merits alone. Much of the Old

146

Testament it quite rejects as belonging to the category of legend and poetry. The New Testament it regards with critical intellectuality and discriminating study. Its advanced scholars doubt the authenticity of any one of the four Gospels. Still the figure of the Christ, his character and life, dominate their thought.

Intellectual Protestantism is profoundly religious, but not in the institutional sense. It still takes the old attitude that the Pope is a mere hold-over from the Imperial pagan ages, a mediæval ecclesiastical figure. But it is not vituperative and negative. It is scholarly and constructive. It holds that spirit produces form; that form does not produce spirit. It insists that every individual must secure for himself the factors of his religion and that nobody can do your thinking for you. Religion is not to be handed out to men on a silver tray, even engraved with the papal arms. Religion is a work for men to do for themselves, and there is no substitute for individual thinking. Protestantism believes in com-

147

plete freedom for the intellect. Much that has been defined and measured by the ancient theologues it dismisses as beyond human knowing. It does not put its trust in external observances but in interior spiritual attainment. It functions in the spirit, not in the machine. It places human charity above correct theological ideas. Just how far it goes in the rejection of ancient values or in the feeling that the revelation of God is progressive, is uncertain. It is decidedly individualistic, and its adherents differ widely in knowledge and attainment.

The old type of Protestantism is a dying cause. It will wane before the advance of education. The new is not yet fully formulated and by no means organized.

But between the extremes of Roman Catholicism and intellectual Protestantism there is still the middle ground of Anglicanism and the Oriental Orthodox churches. Of these the second holds as the fundamental background of the faith to the seven ecumenical councils, those great synods of the early church, in which so many details of doctrine, discipline, and worship were settled. It interprets the Scripture upon that basis, conceiving truly that since the church existed before the New Testament was written and officially chose the books that compose it, the church is the sole authority and guide to its meaning, the creeds a compass in a sea of mystery. For the practical direction of its later affairs the Oriental churches have so much depended upon the direction of the emperors, czars, kings, and princes of the nations in which they have existed that the Oriental Orthodox episcopate has virtually lost its autonomy and its structure is shattered in the event, as in Russia, of a revolution.

I shall hold no brief for Anglicanism, since that is my own position. But it may be said that the Church of England and the English colonies and the Episcopal Church in the United States represent that peculiar quality of illogical structure that is characteristic of the race. On the one hand, the Anglican Church is strictly liturgical

149

and prides itself upon having the episcopate, a priesthood, and diaconate. On the other hand, it professes the Fundamentalist Biblical position for its final authority. It is a creature of the state in the mother country and is controlled by the laity elsewhere. But its scholars are for the most part liberally Modernist and, though it clings to tradition, it is alive to the most advanced critical theories and freely speculative.

There is little prospect that the world at large will accept the theory that Anglicanism is the middle ground appointed by God for the reunion of Protestants and Catholics—the *Via Media*. Its position is too vague and indefinite. Men are moved in history by clear-cut ideas, even when wrong, that can be easily understood and require little elucidation. A carefully balanced position, a yielding to both sides of the question, the compromising accommodations of diplomacy appeal only to the learned and the middle-aged. The *Via Media* is apt to become a line of cleavage.

150

The Orientals, separated from the Western world since the eighth century, are so remote and exotic as to be out of the question. When Pope Eugenius IV, at the Council of Florence in 1439, attempted to adjust the petty theological differences between Roman Catholics and the Orientals—differences of a slight wording in the creed, of the use of unleavened bread in the eucharist, of the kind of images to be venerated in churches—the effort came to little or nothing. They are very much set in their ways. And some of their ways are excellent.

III

Now if Cardinal Newman was right and truth is to be found in extremes, I confess to a bewilderment of choice in the extremes of ecclesiastical ideals before the world. There are many things about Roman Catholicism that make it a very desirable religion. For example, worship. At its best Roman Catholicism presents a

151

'form of worship beautiful, symbolic, dramatic, rich in color and in meaning, hallowed by ages of use in devotion, supremely simple and dignified. Only the jaundiced eyes of race prejudice would hesitate to admire it, and only the tasteless and slovenly ministrations of a careless priesthood can mar it. While Protestant worship at its best is cold, colorless, dull, without inspiration. Why should it be expected, in an age when even the manufacturers of automobiles are compelled to include beauty in the structure of their machines, that people should be content to sit for an hour or more staring at the vapid pipes of a large organ, three impossible plush chairs, and an enormous open Bible on a commonplace stand, while a man in a frock coat tells God the events of the past week and preaches a sermon? Yet this is what the Protestant churches provide as the chief act of worship on Sunday mornings. And the jazzy, hearty type is even worse. It pushes vulgarity to the very extreme. Architecturally, too, the difference is all in favor of the Roman Catholic.

Protestants profess a holy horror of Catholic superstition, of idolatry. Something of this is probably inevitable among the masses of ignorant worshipers. It is not of the essence of the faith. But what is more serious is the general intransigence of the theological position of the papacy. Roman Catholic theologians seem to think it necessary to cling with pleadings and apologies to ideas in religion that no intelligent person at the present time can possibly hold. For example, the literal fall of man. The whole evidence of the study of science is against the doctrine. Yet it is a matter of faith in that church. Why cling to old legends that nobody accepts as literal truths?

"With fullness of knowledge," says Lord Acton, the eminent Roman Catholic historian, "the pleader's occupation is gone and the apologist is deprived of his bread. Mendacity depended on concealment of evidence. When that is at an end, fable departs with it and the margin of legitimate divergence is narrowed." These words were written of history. They might well be pondered by theologians.

Religion may not be presented solely for the edification of intellectual men, but there is no use in alienating them. And the attitude of Roman Catholicism in this regard is perhaps the greatest obstacle to its success. The day is gone when religious obscurantism can avail to stop the free knowledge of mankind. It is due to the fearless and critical study of scholars defying ecclesiastical censure that nearly every advance in scientific knowledge for the benefit of mankind has been attained and given to the world. And this intransigence did not cease at the period of Galileo. It is still with us. The famous Eucharistic Congresses, held by Roman Catholics in some city of the world every year, began with an attempt on the part of Roman Catholic scholars to study the problems connected with sacramental ideas. But what free discussion there was at the first was soon put to silence. The

154

Eucharistic Congresses are now nothing but spectacles for arousing popular devotion and advertising the church. And if during them scholars read papers, they are lost in the clamor, or have become nothing but the most fulsome panegyric.

But after all what has all this theological clamor and ecclesiastical debate to do with actual religion? It is not religion at all. It has perhaps to do with the method of presenting religion, but religion itself is something infinitely greater than churches. It rises over and above them. It is invisible, like the Kingdom of God that cometh not with observation. It belongs to the infinite and the eternal. It is a matter between God and the human soul.

Protestants are right in declaring that spirit precedes form. And Catholics may be right in holding that if a man conforms to the ordinances of religion the church will pull him through to the shores of salvation, though the devil works days and sweats nights trying to destroy his

155

soul. It is all one. The man who is to be saved
must in the end conform himself to the laws
of God, for he cannot know that to which he has
no resemblance. He must reach justice, mercy,
and truth, or be damned. Whatever waits on
the other side of life, it is certain that here at
least the kingdom of God within us cannot be
realized without our aspiration and desire. The
particular theological tenets a man holds, the
forms in which he participates, the church to
which he belongs, count as nothing in comparison to the nature of his actual life in the every-
day world. He is judged not by his creed but
by his acts. His creed may inspire his imagination and affect his character. It must do that,
or he is lost.

Unfortunately it is the curious infirmity of
the human mind to substitute the means for the
end. The institutionalist and the ecclesiastic always seem to emphasize the church rather than
God. The organization, the machinery of religion, too often take the place of religion it-

self. Professionalism is substituted for piety. Loyalty is felt to be loyalty to the formulated systems of men rather than to the truth of God. The religious mind, like the mediæval mind, looks backward. Progressive knowledge is strangled in a skein of meticulous and petty precedents.

IV

President Dwight—he lived in a day when college presidents were still scholars—was right. If there were only one church in the world, it would be necessary for somebody to go out and start another one. Ultimate Truth in religion lies far ahead and we shall be a long time in attaining it. Centuries of patient labor. The clash of conflicting theories. The discovery of new ideas. The elucidation of mystical experiences. The blending of scientific truth with traditional religious emotion. An understanding of the psychology of sanctity. And such progress implies division.

157

To attempt a synthesis of the extremes of recognized theological positions, to unite in a single authoritative body the churches, is a dream similar in kind to the schemes to eliminate poverty, to create a universal language, to destroy capitalism, to perfect governments, to make democracy safe for the world, to determine taste, to reach Utopia. It is the delight of secretaries, the despair of honest men. But it cannot be done.

The best that can be done is to aim at the ideal. It is well to remember that character is to be judged not by what it is but by what it tends to become. Let results take care of themselves.

The World Conference on Faith and Order, held last summer at Lausanne, was a gallant effort to bring about corporate and spiritual church unity by a meeting of the religious leaders of the world for a discussion of the problem. Conceived about the same time as Mr. Ford's Peace Ship, it was destined to have about the same results. Always in the past such appearances of church unity as existed were the result of compulsion by the state. Either persecution, as in the Imperial ages, forced the churches to hold together, or the state itself, theoretically Christianized, as in the Middle Ages and down to modern times, made heresy and schism crimes. The old method worked badly. The thumb-screw, the rack, the fagot did not suffice to compel the church to keep united. Always there were new sects arising. The emperors of old Rome could not stop them. The mediæval kings, aided by the Inquisition, could scarcely keep them down. There were Waldenses, Albigenses, Jacqueries, rebellions. There were even at one time three popes. Finally, the rise of nations, the new learning, discovery, commerce, science, brought about the Reformation and divided the church in Western Europe into the fragments we see to-day. Men began to dig up the sources of religion. They have been examining them with microscopes ever since.

159

But economic pressure, the falling away from religion of great masses of the population of the world, the confusion and dissatisfaction that exist at the present time, the inability of religion to control the waste and passion of life, to maintain peace, are exerting the same effect upon the churches as persecution did in the earlier eras. These things alarm and draw the churches together.

The World Conference on Faith and Order was an historical event of the first importance, though it passed almost unnoticed in the public press of America. The ecclesiastical historians a century hence will acclaim it as significant. It symbolized a need, a condition.

As was expected, the conference accomplished no direct results. Its delegates, drawn from some eighty sects throughout the world, had no authority to commit their churches. They acted merely as individuals. What authority they had came solely from their individual positions as scholars and men of piety. The conference was over-

160

whelmingly Protestant. The Pope refused to go. He not only did not go himself, but it was reported that he ordered that no representative of the Roman Catholic Church, clerical or lay— with the exception of two "unofficial observers" —should even attend as a spectator the meetings of the conference. The Pope knows his book. Why in the world it should have been expected that he would attend passes understanding. At Lausanne the opening meeting was held in a cathedral despoiled by Protestants at the Reformation, the Cathedral of Notre Dame consecrated in 1275 by Pope Gregory X, a place of papal memories. And who could expect the head of the greatest body of Christians in the world, outnumbering all the others put together, to heed the call to unity in an assembly arranged by the Protestant Episcopal Bishop of New York and presided over by the Bishop of Western New York? If the commission had had the tact to ask the Pope to call such a meeting and to preside over it, the outcome might have been

161

different. Certainly the world would have sat up and taken notice.

Such reports on Faith and Order as the various committees made were naturally also Protestant. For example, the recognition as valid of any form of ordination that makes it evident that a man is ordained to the ministry of any church could not fail to disconcert the high-church Anglicans and drew a formal dissent from the Orthodox Orientals present. Here was a shock, indeed. For what is Anglicanism without episcopacy? In short, as in all democratic assemblies, conferences, pourparlers, round-tables and similar talk-fests, where the object is to reach agreement, there was the inevitable necessity of compromise, adjustment, watering-down, concession, acceptance of the lowest common denominator of conviction.

To assert that the courteous spirit and restraint of the members of the conference in their speeches was an evidence of prospective unity is surely a mistake. The disgraceful scenes of

162

earlier assemblies, when clergy flew at each other's throats and anathemas were freely hurled, belong to the ages of barbarism. Civilization and the amenities of modern life sufficiently account for the better manners displayed at the meeting. But the tenacity of opinion, the unyielding convictions, were even at a distance apparent. The majority of those present were able to agree—to differ.

The assembly being Protestant with the exception of the picturesque Orientals was, it must be confessed, rather gray, rather somber, quite lacking in the color, spectacular splendor, pomp and ceremony such as appeal to popular imagination. Its deliberations, couched in the language of esoteric sentimentalism, failed to register in the public press. And since it was a foregone conclusion that every delegate knew beforehand exactly what his own position and that of his own denomination was, as well as what each of the others held, the value of such a conference may be questioned—except that it

163

gave in the heat of summer at a lovely place in Switzerland a gorgeous junket to the commissioners and the secretaries. The conclusions could have been as well arrived at by correspondence. Except for clergymen and the editors of church papers the conference passed without stirring popular interest.

V

Any scheme of corporate unity, then, is beyond the diplomatic skill of even the most astute ecclesiastical leaders. It is not a matter of practical politics. If it is, as is so often asserted, the divine will, then it is on a par with the other great and ultimate ideals. "Be united" can only be compared with "Have all knowledge," "Agree on Ultimate Truth," "Sustain perfect charity," "Be devoid of every prejudice." It belongs to the eternal categories. It is an excellent aim, but a mystical attainment. The individual may have the feeling for it, but he cannot material-

164

ize or demonstrate it. To arrive even at the emotion as a spiritual experience is to transcend all
the churches.[1]

There remains, however, a practical aspect of
the problem in America that ought to be under-
taken, not by impractical idealists, but by ec-

[1] It is often insisted upon that the words in Jno. XVII:21,
"That they all may be one," etc., make it mandatory for
Christians to strive for the organized unity of Christendom.
But in the first place it is doubtful that these actual words
were ever uttered by Jesus. Of St. John's Gospel, Streeter
("Reality" p. 180) says: "The Gospel of John is not a biog-
raphy but a meditation. It is a mystic's interpretation of the
essence of Christianity cast into dramatic form. It should
be read as we read a dialogue of Plato or the book of Job,
that is, for the sake, not of the incidents and situations, but of
the thought they are selected to convey." This is the general
opinion of modern scholars. And in any case, it is evident
that the words of the prayer attributed to Jesus express, not
unity of organization, but unity of spirit in God. As the consciousness of the divine life was in him, and hence was
potential in every man, so he is represented as praying that
this consciousness of unity with God might be realized in
all his followers. This is something quite different from church
unity in the matter of organization, for the organization might
well contain, like the field in the parable, wheat and tares, men
good and evil.

165

clesiastical statesmen. For in this country we have listed some 167 varieties of religion, and at least twenty more not listed. Besides the main and better known divisions, such as the Methodists, Baptists, Presbyterians, Congregationalists, Episcopalians, and Roman Catholics, there are many large communions of earnest Christians banded together and separated from the others, in competition with them. The divisions run largely along racial lines, it is true. The German, the Scandinavian, the Hungarian, the Greek, the Serbian churches witness to the importation of religion along with the national waves of immigration. And even in the Roman Catholic Church the same strains of race are found in the Irish, the Italian, the German, and other groups. But in addition to such divisions, which tend greatly to prevent the assimilation of the foreign-born, there are very many divisions among Protestants based upon progressive or conservative theories or upon the special emphasis of some particular tenet, that foster

166

discord and stimulate destructive competition. We have, for example, such sects as the Six Principle Baptist, the Two-Seed-in-the-Spirit Predestinarians, the Duck River Baptists, the Pilgrim Holiness Brethren. There are two sects of Brethren, Conservative and Progressive, split on the question of whether a man's coat shall have one button or two, the two-buttoners being Progressive. We have the Zarephath, the Pillar of Fire. We have Holy Rollers and Holy Jumpers.

It is probable that nothing much could be done with the smaller and intense groups that specialize on some particular aspect of religion. But with the greater and more important sects something in the way of unity ought to be accomplished. Their theological differences at the present time are very slight. Yet they divide the Christian heritage, split up the faithful, confuse the outsider, and engage in a wasteful and expensive competition for members and money that greatly weakens respect for religion and reduces the ministry of all churches to a condition of poverty and social inferiority. The enormous cost of up-keep, the extravagance of the missionary departments, the overhead of the boards, secretaries, executive secretaries, field secretaries, archdeacons, bishops, presiding elders, and a swarm of paid officials who do no pastoral work but go about laying grievous burdens upon the ministers of all denominations in order that the competition may be kept up, are a few of the evils of the present divided state of the Christian churches in America. In most small towns a single church would suffice for the housing of all who desire to attend religious services. But you will generally find a dozen or more, where one would be fairly strong, struggling to pay their bills and cutting each other's throats in the effort to make one proselyte.

This condition is both disgraceful to America and injurious to our civilization. It presents religion without dignity. The very buildings, the houses of God, show by their inferior architecture the futility of the spirit within. The nation

168

in every other respect rising to heights of accomplishment in this is failing wretchedly. Something practical should be done about it.

Some practical attempts to bring about greater unity among the various Protestant sects have in recent years been made in Canada, Australia, and among the English missions in India. Of these the Canadian effort to unite the Methodist, Congregationalist, and Presbyterian churches is by far the most advanced. The United Church of Canada is now an established fact. The movements in Australia and India are as yet not much beyond the paper stage.

In the United States for the past twenty years, there have been discussions, conferences, resolutions, and even some attempts to bring about at least some measure of reunion among Protestant sects. Little has been accomplished. Every business man interested in the subject realizes the economic value of a merger. The pastors, I think, would in many cases favor it. But the inherited nostalgia for customary forms

169

and habits in religion of the laity, the vested interests, the suspicion and prejudice in relation to other aspects of Christianity, are seemingly irremovable barriers. The varieties of cultural standards and the divergences in moral theories also are obstacles.

There is still the possibility that at some future time the state, in spite of our boasted theories about the separation of church and state, may take over the matter of religion. America may yet have a state church established by law. The history of every nation in the world in the past has shown the advantages as well as the disadvantages of such an arrangement. The state can give a unity, a dignity, an authority to the church such as nothing else in the world can give. And since the same people who compose the state compose the church, the arrangement is convenient and natural. At the present time the churches are impinging more and more upon the province of legislation, insisting more and more that the state put through their programs. The

170

step may be easier than is commonly realized for the reverse process, in some emergency, to take place, and the churches may some day wake up to find themselves a department of the state, rather than its counselor and guide. This has happened before and may happen again.

AN INTERVIEW

At the seaside. Aged-and-Infirm sat on the porch of the hotel. One of those ultra hotels, suitable for millionaires only.

You pay a dollar for an order of boiled potatoes and get one potato at that. Our foreign-born brothers of the dark-browed, Near East variety flit around like sharks looking for tips. Bootleggers' ladies, glittering with diamonds and pearls, swarm in the lounge. Grotesque girls looking like misshapen boys move about in the company of boys looking like misshapen girls. Tennis rackets and golf sticks. Limousines and liveries. You know the sort.

I looked at Aged-and-Infirm's frayed cuffs, rusty clerical suit, rundown-at-the-heels shoes.

"Staying here?" I asked.

"Ya-a-a-s," he replied. "That is, I'm sitting here. I'm really boarding about a mile back

172

from the beach. Much quieter there. And cheaper. I just stopped in here to call on a couple of my parishioners. They're out. So I sat down awhile to rest. Rather nice here. You can see the ocean."

I observed the blue waves and the swept beach. Girls with practically nothing on added a touch of human interest to the picture.

"You see," continued Aged-and-Infirm, "I found out from the chauffeur that the So-and-Sos were staying here. Their chauffeur boards where I do. Of course he could afford a more expensive place, but he's saving up to buy a home, a house of his own. A nice chap, the chauffeur. I never owned a home of my own," he added pensively. "Always lived in rectories."

"But the rectories were fine houses, were they not?" I asked.

"Oh, yes," he said, "on the outside. You see the trouble is that they usually give you a house that is too expensive to run on the salary you get. And when you first come they fix it up. But

173

afterwards they forget you. A house needs some repairs. Things go to pieces after a few years. It gets to be rather dreadful in time in a rectory. Still I don't know but that it is better to live in a shabby house than it is to have the average parochial committee come in once a year and fix your house up in accordance with their ideas."

"I see," said I, changing the subject, "that there is a new commission on getting young men to study for the ministry. What do you think of their work?"

"It would be better," he replied, "if there were a commission formed to make conditions in the ministry less tragic. I could not conscientiously urge any young man to take Holy Orders as things now are. It is to my mind a crime to play upon the enthusiastic idealism of young men to get them to enter a career which under present conditions puts such crippling limitations and handicaps upon ability."

"But surely," said I, "it is a noble profession. What do you mean?"

174

"It is," said he, "a noble profession all right. But the conditions under which it is maintained are far from noble. Any man who goes into the ministry nowadays, unless he has an exceptional genius or has money of his own, is slated for a life of social degradation, painful humiliations, poverty, and constant anxiety."

"But do not the lay boards, the vestries, the trustees, or whatever you call them," I asked, "look out for all your reasonable temporal needs?"

Aged-and-Infirm gave me a pitying glance such as one bestows upon the ignorant.

"The system of lay control of the temporal affairs of churches," he remarked, "is the whole trouble. The average layman on such a board cares little and knows less about the management of a church. He may think that he does, but he does not. He generally has no personal religion himself. If he has any ideas on religion these are for the most part a mere bundle of negations and prejudices. He seldom goes to

175

church. He learns nothing and forgets nothing. He has no actual stake in the success or failure of the church. He gives little. He merely sits pretty and expects the minister to raise the money which he directs the spending of. His chief activity consists of voting down any plan for advancement the minister may devise, of criticism and fault-finding. It becomes the chief business of the Protestant minister in this country to cajole his lay board into letting him do something. The measure of success on the part of the minister is his ability to please. He has no position of independence. He is dependent upon the good-will of his group. This reduces the profession from the prophetical or priestly class to the humiliating position of a mountebank."

"Why, then," I asked, "do not more men leave the ministry and go out and earn an honest living?"

"Easier said than done," replied Aged-and-Infirm. "You see the first ten years the young man gets on fairly well. These are the best years of the profession. He is in demand. The lay boards always hope that he will be the exceptional genius who will make the church go without their having to do anything or pay anything. The young man gets calls. His salary, for a beginner, is better than that of a lawyer or a doctor at that same age. But by the time he has given hostages to fortune, has a family, is habituated to his work so that he cannot readily change, he has passed the zenith of his attractive qualities. Nobody wants him around. He's a pest. A joke for the family dinner-table on Sundays. A thing to be got rid of if possible. Himself crazy to get away.

"It is no wonder that there are hundreds of applicants for every vacancy. And it is no wonder that the type of men going into the ministry becomes lower and lower. We see fewer men at the seminaries and more of those few are men with bad breaths and no chins, men who would fail in any vocation."

"You draw a horrible picture!" I exclaimed.

"It is not so horrible as the reality," he answered. "You see the age has changed. Not only is the old respect for religion and the ministry departed from the earth, but the conditions of church organization are utterly out of date. The systems of church organization we have were devised for the most part, here in America, in the eighteenth century. Like government by conventions, they are out of date. These conventions have no power of initiative. They drift along merely to record the general condition, a sort of jaunting party where the ministers who are successful and the rich laymen pass bouquets to each other and accomplish nothing worth while."

"But we seem to be getting along somehow," I remarked, growing weary of his Jeremiad.

"The overruling providence of God," he exclaimed. "The Christian church has always found that the human element in it is very hu-

178

man. That, however, is no reason why we should not try to improve conditions."

This I was quite willing to admit. Then, to shift the line of thought, I asked Aged-and-Infirm what he had thought about the Dayton trial.

He grinned.

"The old school of mechanistic evolutionists," he began, "had it coming to them. Thirty years ago, when I was a young man, philosophers of this type thought that, because the scientists had made a little progress in finding out the mode of the creative process, they had eliminated all mystery from the universe. They were sheer materialists. There are no longer any philosophical materialists—only what one might call practical materialists. The So-and-Sos, for instance, on whom I came to call and found that they were out, are practical materialists. They have just about reached, in the way of intellectual development, the ideas of thirty years ago. But all modern scholars realize that evolution does not

179

destroy the spiritual content of creation: it increases our perception of it."

"You endorse, then, Mr. Bryan's attack?" I inquired.

"Nonsense!" he exclaimed. "Bryan was attacking a school of thought long since extinct. He assumed that evolution denied the existence of God. As I have said, some of the early evolutionists did deny the existence of God. But at the present time most evolutionists believe in God. Just as all educated people who are religious are also evolutionists."

"But Mr. Bryan surely was an educated man?"

"No man who believes in the literal account of the creation in the book of Genesis is educated. Such an interpretation belongs to children and savages. It is a queer thing that in this country we have so many otherwise sensible people who are in their theology so crudely literal. It is like the belief that the earth is flat."

"But you yourself were taught just that when

180

you were a theological student, were you not?"

"Never," he replied. "They stuck out against evolution as long as they could in favor of a particular creation, but before even my time they had modernized. All scholars knew this, but the idea is just reaching the masses. It is the adjustment of their imagination to the broader view that is creating the present revolution in the religious world. People are not able to change their religious ideas quickly. It takes a long time. It creates temporary unbelief."

"Is that what you mean by calling the So-and-Sos practical materialists?"

"Yes; somewhat. They have lost their old religious ideas. They can no longer believe in the anthropomorphism of the Bible. But they haven't the time or the brains to work into a conception of a more spiritual idea. They still hang onto the church. Mr. So-and-So is a vestryman. Force of habit. But they attend services less and less and religion has no real hold upon them. I can't teach them anything. Since So-and-So made his money they think they know everything there is to know anyway. Besides, I'm rather a dull preacher."

"I'm sure you're not," I said courteously, though to tell the truth he had bored me horribly in the pulpit.

"Yes, I am," he affirmed. "I was brought up to think that people would go to church, not to hear a sermon, but to worship. Nowadays they do not go at all unless it is to hear either a good sermon or some good music. It is only the Roman Catholics who have any ideas about worship, and they're fast losing them in this country, I hear."

At this point a splendid limousine drove up to the hotel entrance. Aged-and-Infirm recognized it as belonging to the So-and-Sos and bowed to the chauffeur.

"A really religious man," he whispered. "I happen to know that he gives more to his church than his employer does to his own. He is a Catholic."

"Through fear of the priest?" I suggested.

"Rot!" said Aged-and-Infirm. "He fears nobody. Is a great friend of the priest. He really loves his religion."

It was at this point that the So-and-Sos came out of the hotel. They saw but ignored Aged-and-Infirm. The old man muttered something about having been told that they were out a few minutes before, and got up slowly to make his way back to his boarding-house a mile from the beach.

"At least," I encouraged him, "you have your pension to look forward to when the time comes."

For some reason this seemed to strike the old man as funny. He limped off, chuckling to himself and muttering something about the price of cigars.

THE BIOLOGY OF RELIGION

A LARGE number of people, disturbed by the present religious revolution, are asking for a constructive program. They desire to know, in the loosing from old moorings, in what direction to turn. What features out of the past should be conserved? What is fundamental and essential? What experience of religion is possible? How shall we regard the church? What shall we think of Christ? In what degree is morality affected? To the old values that are to be conserved what new features should be added?

It must be admitted that up to the present time the work of revolution has been mainly destructive. Perhaps the time has come to attempt the outline of some of the constructive features of religion in the future.

I

On Easter day, 1754, at Colmar, M. François Marie Arouet, having first confessed to a Capuchin friar, received the Sacrament. This has been represented as an act of irreverence and hypocrisy, painful to believers and harmful to his own reputation. After the service he sent to the Capuchin convent a present of a loin of veal and a dozen bottles of wine. And some have interpreted this as an evidence that he regarded the ceremony with contempt.[1] But at the time M. Arouet was sixty years old. He had just escaped from most painful experiences in Prussia. Permission to return to his native land had been denied him. He was very ill. He thought that he was dying. A sea of troubles seemed ready to engulf him. He did not know where to turn. It is possible that he performed this action with as sincere a purpose as his flippant and critical nature permitted. The present he sent the priests

[1] Tallentyre.

185

was no more than what any well-disposed and considerate person of his rank and fortune would have given at such a time, a proper and usual courtesy.

François Marie Arouet de Voltaire was not an irreligious man. On the contrary. Much as he hated superstition, bigotry and ignorance, he had respect even for the conventional religious customs of the time and place in which he lived. He numbered many of the clergy—who purchased and read his books even when shocked by them—among his friends. Did not the Pope himself, to whom he dedicated his "Mahomet," send him a fragment of the hair shirt of St. Francis of Assisi? Did he not build a church on his estate and set the example of assisting at mass to his tenants and guests on Sundays and festivals? It is even recorded that once from the pulpit he preached a sermon against stealing. As lord of the manor he was always specially censed at the service. He sent his servants

186

out of the room when his guests began to talk atheism. Some of the radicals of his day denounced him as a bigot since he declined to be classed as an atheist. "Si Dieu n'existait pas il faudrait l'inventer," said he.

However sardonic, contemptuous, cynical, critical, mocking, sarcastic, denunciatory, vindictive, vituperative, and bitter, he was not scornful of religion itself. What he hated was the abuse of the machinery of religion as an instrument of oppression. If he made war against priestcraft and autocratic ecclesiastical authority, against obscurantism and the spirit of persecution, it was that he might rescue truth from the *infamy* of religious intolerance—*écrasez l'infâme*.

Voltaire has been regarded as the devil's own instrument for the ruin of faith. It has taken mankind a century and a half to realize that in fact he has contributed more to the enlightenment, liberty, and intellectual honesty of the world than a whole wilderness of preachers. The destruction of error is the first step in the discovery of truth.

II

The critical skepticism of the eighteenth century laid the foundation of the work of religious readjustment which has culminated in our own day. At that time the theories of Copernicus and of Newton had begun to affect the imagination of the more learned of the race. It was realized that the earth is not the center of the universe. Man became a pygmy, an insect. The deists, inheriting anthropomorphic ideas of God, based on the language of Scripture and the pictures of mediæval artists who represented the Eternal Father as an old man with white whiskers, pushed God out of the universe. They could not find Him with their telescopes.

For those who conceive of God as a person, an individual, inhabiting the universe, such a consequence is inevitable. But there is another

188

and less material conception of the deity not un-congenial to theology. That is the idea that God is spirit, that He is everywhere, that He is not a person though He has personality. It is possible to find such a definition even in the Bible. The cosmic consciousness of the mystic and the philosophy of a Spinoza alike took refuge in such ideas of the deity and religion could still present its apologetic to a world that had gone through both an intellectual and a social revolution in consequence of the discoveries of astronomy. If God exists outside of time and space, if He is the Creative Spirit of the universe, if it is possible to have any faith in Him at all, why not conceive of Him as did Tennyson:

Closer is he than breathing, and nearer than hands and feet.

In the doctrine of divine immanence God returned to His universe. Faith revived. It was a triumph for belief. God was no longer merely

189

to be thought of as in the universe. The universe was in God.

The attack in the form of ridicule and criticism of the Bible which accompanied this preliminary skirmish between religion and science was of the superficial type to be found in the works of Voltaire, Paine, and (later) Ingersoll. It consisted in pointing out the inconsistencies, inaccuracies, improbabilities, and immoralities contained in the Old Testament. There were more than enough of these to shake any theory of verbal inspiration. The Higher Criticism completed the work by demonstrating the very human character of the composition of the books. To those whose theology rested solely upon the authority of the Book the effect has been devastating. But to those who regarded the Book as merely an instrument for the teaching of moral and spiritual truths such criticism made little difference in their religious convictions. On the contrary, it made the Book only the more interesting. It showed, indeed, the human side of Hebrew literature, but it also brought out the superiority of Hebrew ideals in religion to the pagan cults of the parallel periods. The values of the wisdom literature stood out only the more clearly. The truths remained unscathed, standing on their own intrinsic merits. Spiritual and moral truths were to be accepted not merely because the Bible said them, but the Bible retained its unique position in literature because it set forth so many moral and spiritual values. In short, the seat of authority was shifted from a Book to the consensus of human opinion. *Securus judicat orbis terrarum,* as St. Augustine said in another connection. The Bible still holds its interest. It is read as much as ever. In the light of criticism it has simply become more interesting. Its lofty ideals and hidden mysteries still fascinate the studious and the spiritual mind. In pointing out the human elements, the defects, absurdities, contradictions, and errors of fact, the Bible has lost nothing of its sublimity of thought or the beauty of its ideals.

The next great shock to the religious imagination came in the nineteenth century in the discoveries of geology, anthropology, and biology —evolution. In America the effect of these discoveries has just reached the masses. It was felt and is felt yet even by some intelligent people that the theory of evolution, with its survival of the fittest and its age-long processes in the origin of species and the descent of man, would move God from any participation in the creative development of the universe. It was forgotten that even the early Christian fathers had regarded the "days" in Genesis as great periods of time. That the earlier chapters of the Bible are poetical accounts of creation and not scientific treatises did not occur to such thinkers any more than it occurs to the crude intelligence of those state legislators who in this country have passed anti-evolution bills.

But quite generally in Europe and increasingly in this country it is realized that the discovery of the processes of creation, like the dis-

192

covery of the vastness of the universe, does not remove the mystery. It rather increases it. As the heavens declare the glory of God so the growth and operations of the inscrutable secrets of life but emphasize the ineffable wisdom and power of the omnipotent and omniscient Being we call God. That there is such a thing as personality in the Creative Principle appears when we consider the civilizations, libraries, literature, art, and science that are the result of the personalities we call men. What is found in the effect must inhere in the Cause.

It is as unthinkable that legislative enactment should stay the acceptance of evolution as that the acceptance of such a theory should eliminate belief in a Living God.

A still further menace to the old-fashioned religious imagination, and one that threatens even greater disruption to the interests of accepted theology, however, has just recently appeared upon the horizon of thought. This will perhaps be more revolutionary than any of its scientific predecessors. The new psychology asserts and proves with great plausibility that the will "is not the master in its own house." Schopenhauer in his day approached this discovery. His "will" is in reality merely "wish." The new psychology makes it clear that man is governed in action and in character by desire. The will is but the instrument of desire. And the theory of complexes makes it clear that we are controlled by hidden emotions the origin and nature of which we but dimly perceive, if we perceive them at all. The effect of this new discovery cannot yet be measured, but it is certain that it will revolutionize many of the ideas people have entertained about sin, just as evolution has destroyed forever the old doctrine of the Fall of Man as a literal fact connected with the eating of an apple. Sin is no longer the deliberate choice of evil by a wicked will but the emergence of sweeping desire that is dominant over the will, the more restrained the more violent.

It is perhaps too early to estimate the effect

194

of this new teaching upon conventional and accepted religion. Many people have not even heard of it and most others have but scanty conceptions regarding it. We shall hear more of it later on as its full implications become clear. So far work on the complex has been confined chiefly to a study of the perverse effects of certain stimuli upon the emotions. But I venture the suggestion that it will be found, like the other scientific discoveries, to be a benefit rather than a harm to true religion. For if the emotions can be affected in an adverse fashion, they can also be affected in the direction of positive virtues. There can be put into the feeling nature the necessary counter-irritants, the idea of courage against fear, of hope over against despair.

III

Such intellectual values as the above may disturb minds closed to the advance of knowledge, destroy some features of antique theologies and

195

upset the dogmas of certain churches. They cannot affect the essential experience of religion.

For as there is a biology of health, so there is a biology of religion. Indeed, religion and health are bound together, inseparable, parts of one and the same thing. Like health, religion may be directed and regulated by authority, or it may be refined, improved, and benefited by intelligence. In its essence, however, it cannot be altered. It is the same essentially in all religions, churches, creeds, cults, beliefs, orthodox or heterodox; whether one is in the true faith or is a heretic, schismatic, dissenter, apostate, backslider, an idolater, fanatic, bigot, nonconformist, sectarian or pagan, a Jew or a gentile, a Turk, a heathen, a pantheist, a Brahmin or a Parsee, a Sufi or a Gymnosophist, a fire-worshiper or a Buddhist, a Thug or a Rosicrucian, a Modernist or a Fundamentalist.

Walt Whitman, in some admirable verses, expresses the essential unity of religious experience.

196

"My faith is the greatest of faiths, and the least of
faiths,

Enclosing worship ancient and modern, and all between ancient and modern,

Believing I shall come again upon the earth after five
thousand years,

Waiting responses from oracles, honoring the Gods,
saluting the sun,

Making a fetish of the first rock or stump, pow-
wowing with sticks on a circle of obis,

Helping the lama or brahmin as he trims the lamps
of the idols,

Dancing yet through the streets in a phallic procession—rapt and austere in the woods, a gymnosophist,

Drinking mead from the skull-cup—to Shastas and
Vedas admirant—minding the Koran,

Walking the teokallis, spotted with gore from the
stone and knife, beating the serpent-skin drum,

Accepting the Gospels—accepting him that was crucified, knowing assuredly that he is divine,

To the mass kneeling, or the puritan's prayer rising,
or sitting patiently in a pew."

The history and ordinances of religion paral-

197

lel the history and ordinances of health. Among primitive people there was no distinction between salvation for the body and salvation for the soul. The sanitary laws of the Jews and the miracles of healing among the Christians show the unity of the relationship of religion and health. The physiological consequences of sin are still offered as an evidence of the wrath of an offended deity. The popularity of modern religious healing cults, of Christian Science for example, indicates the closeness of the ideas of health and religion in the mind of multitudes.

All very reasonable and natural. Health is a matter of feeling. You *feel* well or ill. Religion equally is a matter of feeling. The believer will *feel* serene, exalted, justified, sustained, comforted, encouraged, consoled, courageous, strengthened, sustained, fearless, zealous, calm, contented, kindly, joyful, happy (*i. e.*, blessed) so long as he is convinced that he is in secure relations with his God. And, on the other hand, he will *feel* unhappy, troubled, frightened, remorse-

198

ful, despairing, if he is persuaded that he has incurred the enmity of the divine majesty.

Moreover, it is well known that the effect of such depressing thoughts upon the nervous system and the body is injurious. You can change the chemical character of the blood by an adverse thought, lessen the secretions of the glands, decrease the beating of the heart and the respiration of the lungs, poison yourself, by fear or anger. Likewise, it is possible to benefit health of body by the impression of thoughts of joy and contentment.

Every religion possesses this quality. No form of belief has a monopoly in it. From the Seven Demons of the Babylon mystery to the most calm and dignified aspect of modern Protestantism, insofar as there is a reality of faith, there will be emotion.

When Oliver Goldsmith lay dying, his physician noticed that the pulse of his patient was much more rapid than his condition warranted. He thereupon asked Goldsmith whether there were not something troubling his conscience. Goldsmith replied that there was.

Religious emotion runs all the way from the terrible fears engendered by the taboo of savage priesthoods and the Christian Inquisition—fears of impending punishments and judgment to come which have been known to cause death—to the enthusiastic zeal that engenders the spirit of persecution out of jealousy for the greater glory of God and to the ecstasies of saints and mystics, the devotion that throws life itself away in the cause of religion. And because emotion is so definitely physical it also accounts for the sensual features so often found in primitive religions, in some phases of Oriental mysticism, in the phallic worship of the Mediterranean cults and as an accompaniment of modern revivalism.

IV

Owing to the tremendous emotional power of religious ideas, therefore, it is extremely important that these ideas be considered in a spirit of dispassionate criticism. There are many kinds of religion. Some are better than others. The judicious will choose the best or make selection of those features that are best out of the variety at hand.

There are two ways of regarding the advance of civilization and the increase of human knowledge: progress may be considered as a revelation, a part of the creative energy of God leading men onward and upward in the course of the ages; or it may be thought of as the discovery of man unaided by divine power. The Hebrews conceived of witty inventions as revealed by God. The Greeks, as the legend of Prometheus indicates, felt that man had wrested the secrets of nature from the jealous gods. The majority of religions postulate a revelation. However the more worldly members may regard the knowledge men have gained through discovery or invention as something found out by man himself, it is true that the Christian churches practically all hold that the foundations of their faith rest upon revelation.

The professional ministry, the special pleaders, the paid apologists of the churches, for the most part foster this idea. Both their training and their office make it necessary that they should do so. It has always been the function of the priesthoods of all religions to shroud with a cloud of glory, with legend and the atmosphere of miracle, the commandments and creeds which they taught. It has followed that each religion, each church, each sect, has been presented to its membership as having the fullness of truth and the divine approval for each and every particular of its creed, its form and its methods. If others are tolerable at all, it is merely because they have portions and fragments of that special and approved truth, that is the unique possession of God's own, the elect, the chosen. The emotions of religious enthusiasm and zeal resulting from the holding of such an opinion are intense. They inevitably result

202

in the development of a spirit of superiority, a megalomania, a holier-than-thou attitude, a strong proselyting propaganda, bigotry and intolerance, bitterness and persecution. As every one knows, the history of Christianity, in spite of the character and words of its founder, has been disgraced for ages with the record of crimes, murders, and wars as a consequence of this theory of special revelation.

Let no one suppose that such a spirit is confined to the religious emotions of the Middle Ages. It exists today quite as much as it ever did. One can find expression of it in every sect in Christendom. It breaks out in American life from time to time in great movements like the Ku Klux Klan and is met by proclamations from a thousand Catholic pulpits. It finds expression in various forms of legislation and attempted legislation. If it is held in check at all, that is because so many sensible and educated people who no longer attend churches at all do not accept the theory that God has given any special revelation in religion any more than He has in any other department of knowledge. And in a divided religious world these hold the balance of power. It is fortunate for the peace of the nation.

Nevertheless, we are at a point in the education of mankind where a synthesis of the two ways of looking at the advance of knowledge may be attempted. Biblical criticism has made it abundantly clear that the thunders of Sinai and the finger of God writing the Decalogue on two tables of stone were but the priestly method of presenting for popular consumption the series of rules for human conduct and the maintenance of the social order collated from the codes of already civilized peoples with the additions necessary for the special Hebrew ethic. But apart from the legends the Decalogue is still a work of genius. As such it corresponds with all other works of genius throughout time.

Consider the benefit to mankind of such inventions in the primitive world as the bow and arrow, the use of fire, the domestication of the cow, the making of bread, cheese, and wine, the planting of the olive. They were works of genius. Are they less important than the giving of a law for the establishment of a nation? Are they not in their way equally valuable? Equally the gift of God? Why eliminate God, the Creative Principle, from the process of development? Why confine the idea of revelation to religion? Are not the laws of health quite as much the laws of God as the laws of prayer?

As the world advances in knowledge the importance of laws—physical, moral, and spiritual—becomes the criterion of values. And since there can be but one source of the universal law, why not recognize that source, both in religion and in life, as God? The separation of religion from life, the idea of a special and peculiar revelation in religion and a very human and ordinary attainment of knowledge in life, is unphilosophical. Why perpetuate an error? And why eliminate the idea of God? Where do ideas

205

come from? How does the genius add the increment of novelty to knowledge? "How to the singer cometh the song?"

It is very interesting and suggestive to inquire into the way in which some modern inventor, artist or musician gets his ideas. From the published statements of Mr. Edison and from the accounts given by others, it seems to me that they get their ideas by a method which corresponds very closely to prayer and meditation. They may not call themselves religious men. They may and generally do repudiate the idea of a personal God. They are far from being anthropomorphists. Their imaginations do not picture a vast Man with long white whiskers sitting on a cloud in some remote corner of the universe ordering the worlds. But the same may be said of many religious people who yet profess belief in God. When they seek an idea for a new invention, a composition, a work of art, they may not adopt a conventional attitude of prayer. After studying the work already done along the same line, they look inside themselves to see whether something new may not be added to that which they already have. It comes across, they say. The kingdom of God is within them and they seek to draw out of the Great Reservoir of Truth that which they need for their purposes. This may not be religion, but it is divine. If they do not recognize the church, it might be well for the church to recognize them. They would make very good members. They work miracles. They are the modern saints. *Gloria in excelsis Deo.*

V

It is a law of biology that life develops the body and it is a conclusion of mysticism that spirit precedes form. The oyster makes the shell; the shell does not make the oyster. Mind produces machinery; machinery does not produce life.

The age-long error of ecclesiastics has been

that the church and the mechanism of religious propaganda will by their own vitality bring forth spiritual fruit. But Annas and Caiaphas were the products of the Jewish church and they decreed death to the spirit of the New Law. Whereas every vitalizing germ of life even in Christianity itself has come, not from the outworn and dying forms of ecclesiasticism, but from the spirit of an individual illuminated from above. Benedict of Nursia, St. Francis of Assisi, St. Ignatius, at Subiaco, at the *Portiuncula,* at Manresa; Martin Luther at Wittenberg, John Calvin at Geneva; these men turned the course of history in its channels. What they did they did in very much the same fashion used by the inventors, discoverers, poets, musicians, and artists who started a new mode and moved the world in a new direction. Long nights in prayer and meditation. Days in critical study of the existing conditions and needs. Waiting for the revelation. The mystical and silent voice. The light within. A new idea. A new hope. A new application of old principles. Theologians and divines have dressed up their spiritual experiences in legendary accounts of special miracles. In reality they differed not at all from the experiences of similar character in the secular sphere. The application of common sense, thought, and intelligence to a practical problem, together with that mysterious added element, the new idea, that comes as a gift from Beyond.

The ecclesiastical organism that follows and is developed from this gift of a new life can only imitate. It attempts to reproduce by copying the lines of the master. It molds in the form he set. But reproduction without renewed vitalization is a deteriorating process. The forms do not fit presently the changed conditions and the new needs. The law of imitation affects spiritual movements as well as sociological movements. They tend to settle down toward sterility and death. They require the fertilization of new ideas and new methods to keep them alive.

Substitution of the means for the end is a

common weakness of human nature. But there is no institution in which this has been done more persistently and completely than in the Christian church. Loyalty, conformity, and adhesion to the institution has been preached as the final test of true religion for nigh two thousand years. Preachers and theologians have so constantly asserted this as an ideal that even the genius of great saints and reformers has been met with a war of opposition the clamor of which has disgraced the history of the western world. It has resulted in the multiplication of the machinery of the churches.

In reality the elements of the Christian religion are of an extreme simplicity. People who have once learned them do not need to be continually reminded of them. An occasional reminder suffices. And it is probably for this reason that so many intelligent people so seldom go to church. They do not require to be told the same things over and over again. Taught the elements of religion in childhood, they feel that they can be trusted to apply them in later life without being exhorted week by week to do so. It is not that they despise the churches or are hiding away from the denunciation of their vices. They are merely bored by dull iteration and have something else to do. Meticulous observance of ecclesiastical ordinances is not always an evidence of virtuous conduct in the week-day world or the criterion of excellence of character.

Nevertheless, the churches have something worth while to do. In a measure and with many human handicaps they do it. Their function is to teach the young and the ignorant and to remind all men of the essential features of religion. They can or should throw light on the problems of life and supply hope, consolation, and courage to those in the struggle. Their benediction offers the peace of God which passes all understanding to the troubled soul. Divided and top-heavy with organization they stagger in the task.

211

In spite of this, in some measure they do it. For this they deserve support in both attendance and money. If the churches were united, nationally or otherwise, they would exercise great influence. The small, divided groups cannot rise above the ability of those who direct their affairs. And yet experience proves that a monopoly becomes, like all other human institutions, oppressive and the foe to liberty. If church unity were to be brought about, it would probably be necessary to break it up in the interests of progress and freedom.

If it is the business of the preacher to inculcate correct ideas of religion, it is the province of worship to produce good feeling. Good feeling is the more important, since it may be assumed that the average congregation has the opportunity of ascertaining the truths of religion by individual thought. There can be no doubt that a solemn and majestic act of worship creates a deep and beneficent impression upon the emotional nature.

VI

Man stands at the apex of the visible creation amid the vast eternities of time and space. Before him rises the significant figure of the Christ. No human life compares with the bright and beautiful history of this young Galilean teacher. Greater than Confucius or the Buddha, more persuasive than the dreams of Plato or the arguments of Aristotle, his words have had more effect upon history than the marching of the armies of Alexander or the conquests of Cæsar. The famous men in the records of the race pale beside him.

Leaving aside the slender story of his miraculous birth and the discordant accounts of his resurrection, by which he was accounted an equal to the demigods of the pagan mysteries of the Mediterranean littoral of his day, and paying no heed to the creeds, decrees, conciliar decisions, hair-splitting definitions of theologians, by which it was attempted to reach an exact ac-

213

count of his relation to the divine essence, as a result of which he has become in many minds a kind of second God, it is of the highest value to consider merely his human character and the records of his teaching. As a man he stands unique.

Jesus was forceful—without violence. He was convivial—without laxity. He was austere—without acerbity. He was intellectual—but not ineffectual. And these four sociological types of character he combines in a harmonious whole in all of their excellencies and none of their defects. Hence, as a man he is the wonder and admiration of the world.

His teaching was profound and penetrating. In the moral and spiritual sphere he is admittedly without a rival. Whatever traditional sources he may have used he gave a colorful simplicity and an added touch to age-long wisdom. The modern critic may conclude that he had what the psychoanalyists would call a complex in that he was convinced that his interior

life was illuminated by the divine indwell-
ing and the egoisms attributed to him are of
the most astounding sort. He was one with the
Father. But there is no reason to think that the
mind of Jesus received its illumination in any
way different from that of other men. As in the
cases of the inventors, discoverers, artists, and
musicians cited, the nights of prayer and meditation, the long preparation invited to the clear
mind of a supreme genius an influx of supernal
light.

Too great an emphasis has been put in the
past upon the birth, the resurrection, the ascension, the theological scheme of salvation, in the
supposed effects of these objective facts, in the
esoteric theories of his relation to God in the hy-
postatic union. Men have been persuaded that
salvation consisted in the contemplation of and
faith in these features of biographical and theological formularies. But the gospel of Jesus was
not a gospel of this sort. It was the good news
of the kingdom, the realm of God which cometh

not with observation, the consciousness of the fact that the divine energy and the divine law that moves the stars in their courses and makes the outgoing of the morning to praise Him is within us.

What he was and what he experienced in cosmic consciousness and in conformity to divine purpose must be open to the experience and conformity of every man. In kind if not in degree we may become as he was.

VII

There is then a Biology of Religion quite as truly as there is a biology of health. So widespread a phenomenon as religion in human life merits the consideration of scientific thought. There are certain laws discoverable in religious experience.

And religion should not be thought of as apart from life in its general aspect. The same God who governs the operations of nature is the

God whom we worship in our churches. There is no place where He is not. Those who consider religion solely a business for Sunday and a matter of special occasion, who make a distinction between the sacred and the secular, may justify their position on the ground of convenience in thought or technical definition. But to fail to import the idea of religion into every aspect of life is to lose the sense of unity in existence and to miss the application of the creative process in the experience of daily affairs.

TO MEN OF GOOD-WILL

"CAPTAIN," said I to the mate. "Sir to you," replied the mate.

"Will you smoke?" said I, handing him a cigar.

"That will I," he answered, taking the weed.

You make no mistake calling a mate "captain." He has invariably been captain—of something or other in the way of craft. He hopes to be a captain quite soon again. He is inwardly persuaded that he would make a better captain than the "old man" below taking a snooze. Therefore the title touches his pet complex. It soothes and stimulates him. He will begin to spin.

Thus it was that, under the broad and starry southern sky on a moonlit night, the sails drawing taut in the steady trade, the vessel lifting evenly over the enormous swells, I heard the story of how the doctors administer the "black

bottle" to obstreperous and moribund patients
in hospitals. I listened to accounts of sword-
fish rising out of the water and stabbing sea-
men in small boats over the gunwales. I was told
of coast-guards who retired from the service as
millionaires after incredibly short seasons in the
twelve-mile limit. Of gunmen along the docks of
New York who would do a man in for twenty-
five dollars. Of a voodoo queen in Haiti. Of
steering by dead-reckoning on the Grand Banks.
Of a tribe on the West African coast that still
eat "long pig." Of priests in the South Seas
who walk on red-hot stones. Of the sailor's long-
ing to leave the sea and settle down ashore. Tales
for the marines. The tale of a tub.

That inferior constellation, the Southern
Cross, glittered above the horizon. In the ecliptic
swam the half-moon. And Jupiter was rising in
the east.

"I have heard of people," said I, "who have
been able to see four of the moons of Jupiter
with the naked eye."

"Moons of Jupiter?" he queried vaguely.

I remarked on the size of the planet in comparison with our own satellite. A lecture by Einstein to a girls' school.

"Humph!" he exclaimed, "it looks smaller to me."

Eight bells struck.

"I'm goin' below," said the mate. "I allus read a chapter of the Good Book afore I turn in."

It was Christmas eve, and I was conscious of the peculiar emotion that so often takes possession of the soul on that occasion. A nostalgia for the simple pure joys of childhood. The quiet serenity of home. The nip of cold in the northern air. The first fall of light snow. The glitter of the stars in a higher latitude. The kindly greetings. The swarm of memories. Of friendships. Of shyly prepared gifts. Of the silent gathering of the congregation for the midnight mass. The white altar. The soft light of the candles. The clear ringing of bells in the distance. The aro-

matic scent of the incense. The odor of pine-
trees. The outburst of Christmas carols and
hymns. The racial happiness of the Day. There
is a sadness. A hesitation. A doubt. A tug between the emancipated and critical intellect and
the inherited emotions, the complexes of childhood. A question of relative values. Is the world
better off for its sophistication, its loosing from
the moorings of a simple unquestioning faith,
its investigation of dogmatic authority, its acceptance of new conceptions? At such a time
as this the question comes. Do the stars have
any other purpose than to shine?

If some of the mate's yarns had seemed to
me a trifle high in color, no doubt some of my
speculations, or even scientific facts, would have
seemed to him miching mallecho, subversive of
all accepted truth.

I was ruminating over the problem of it when
the professor came blundering up the companion-
way. The professor never did get his sea-legs on

221

during the whole voyage. Perhaps he carried too
many heavy ideas in the ballast of his brain.

"Come down and play a game of chess," said
the professor. "I have invented a new gambit,
and you shall be the first victim."

"You talk," said I, "better than you play."

"We can talk at the same time," said he.

We descended into the cabin and pegged the
men into their holes on the board, drew for
colors and began. I outlined my incredulity in
some of the mate's yarns and the mate's blank
unbelief in the simple facts of astronomy.

"Pooh!" said the professor after he had set
the trap of his new gambit, which was not in
the least new but only the old queen's pawn
dodge. "The mate's stories are all true enough.
But as for seeing the moons of Jupiter with the
naked eye, who ever heard of such a thing but
yourself?" He peered at me through his enormous horn-rimmed spectacles.

"Besides," he continued after I had taken the
pawn, "people always believe what they wish to

believe. There is no such thing as the will to believe. There is only the desire to believe. Freud is right. The will is bent and twisted like a reed in the wind by the emotions, the passions, as they used to be called, the desires. It is desire that rules belief, not will. And the reason, if one may make a distinction in the faculties of the brain, is but the instrument which justifies choice and decision."

"Do you mean to tell me," I asked, advancing the red knight, "that the multitudes on land tomorrow who will attend the Christmas services in their churches are actuated solely by desire and not through conviction based on a religious teaching that controls the will and regulates the emotions?"

"Christmas!" said he. "Bah! The Saturnalia. A pagan festival. Goes back to the very dawn of history. The first day after the winter solstice in the northern hemisphere. The first day their crude instruments could detect the return of the sun. Joy to the world. The sun-god was coming back. There would be another spring. Food. I tell you it's in the blood. Part of the race inheritance. A mob complex."

"But the will," I hazarded, eyeing the dangerous location of his white queen. "Granted that the will is swayed by the emotions, it is at least a matter of volition whether one encourages the religious emotion by allowing the imagination to dwell upon the religious idea of the Incarnation. For you will admit, I suppose, that imagination affects the emotions?"

He looked up from the board, pulled out his meerschaum pipe, and lighted it before replying.

"It is something like this vessel," he remarked. "The wind moves it along by pressing upon the sails. The wind corresponds to the emotions that move the man. You cannot order the wind to change. But the helm directs the course. You can direct the vessel by turning the helm so that it will move even against the wind—indirectly. Well, the helm may be compared to the will. That is to say, you can put ideas into your imagination by what appears at least to be an act of volition, and the consequent emotions will move you in the direction suggested by the ideas imagined, provided they soak deep enough into the nervous system, or what some people call the subconscious mind. But why you make the choice of the particular idea, and whether you really do make such a choice or are persuaded to it by some deeper emotion, is yet again another matter."

"At any rate," I persisted, removing my king's bishop from a position of imminent danger, "you will not deny that the Christmas story appeals to the imagination of multitudes of people and, since it affects their emotions in a religious direction, has a religious value?"

"Value!" he exclaimed, attacking my queen with a rook. "Value for primitive folk, the uneducated, savages, and children. Value for a certain phase of the race's development. Yes. But for me the day itself has no significance whatever. There is no evidence worth considering that Jesus was born on the twenty-fifth of December. It is certain that he was not born nineteen hundred and twenty-six years ago at least by two or maybe four years. Besides, the theological doctrines of orthodoxy distress me. Who can make anything of the *Logos* of Philo that the author of the fourth Gospel adopted? What modern philosopher thinks in the terms of the mediæval schoolmen—nature, substance, hypostasis, person, procession, generation, relation—in the sense in which they used them? Bolstered up by the anathemas of conciliar decrees. It reminds me of that monk in Browning:

> "There's a great text in Galatians,
>   Once you trip on it, entails
> Twenty-nine distinct damnations,
>   One sure, if another fails."

Can you affect people's imaginations by asserting something that their imaginations are incapable of grasping? Can you control the will of free men by theological threatenings?"

226

I castled. It was necessary. His queen and two knights were bearing down upon my line.

"As a matter of fact," he continued, "the ordinary teaching you hear in the churches is little better than sheer heresy. Most Christians conceive of Jesus as a kind of second God. Indeed Justin Martyr who was the chief advocate of the *Logos* doctrine at Rome in the third century, spoke of a 'second God.' Your Nicene Creed and your ordinary preacher give the idea that the second person—meaning an individual like ourselves—disengaged himself from the tangle of the eternal Trinity, came literally down from a local heaven, and was born as a child. They worship the babe in the manger. His hands are the hands of God. His tears are the tears of God. Now for my part I shall refuse to worship a baby."

"Because perhaps," said I, "you never had one."

"Ah, yes," he replied, wiping his spectacles, "my mother—"

227

"Women do," I suggested, "in a way."

"They do indeed," he answered. "I admit it."

For some moments the strategy of the game kept us both from speaking. It was my move, and the professor's king's knight's pawn had advanced to a position in support of his queen's bishop that interrupted my plan of attack. One of those serious pauses that every chess-player knows. The professor leaned back in his chair confident of the strength of his position. Outside on the deck I could hear the creaking of the cordage in the blocks. At the port-holes I could catch glimpses of the waves, their spray turned to silver in the moonlight. Presently I saw the opening and moved. Once more we took up the thread of our talk.

"But aside from the theology," I insisted, pressing the advantage I perceived on the board in an attack I had started with a rook and my two bishops, "is there not something about the day that merits consideration even from so learned a person as yourself?"

He put up his hand as if to ward off both the compliment and the strategic attack of my pieces.

"I will quote you," said he, "a passage from Chamberlain. I learned it by heart because it is so admirably expressed and so true. In his 'Foundations' he says: 'No battle, no change of dynasty, no natural phenomenon, no discovery possesses a significance which can be compared with that of the short life upon earth of the Galilean. His birth is, in a sense, the beginning of history. The nations that are not Christian, such as the Chinese, the Turks and others, have no history; their story is but the chronicle on the one hand of ruling houses, butcheries and the like, and on the other represents the dull, humble, almost bestially happy life of millions that sink in the night of time without leaving a trace.' "

"Excellent," I exclaimed. "And how do you account for it?"

"Why," answered the professor, "I account

229

for it primarily in view of his character. Jesus was not the androgynous figure of the church windows, the anemic, unreal being of the ecclesiastical artists. He was a man. You might call him, if you like, The Man. You will find that scientific sociology makes four types of character: the forceful, the convivial, the austere, and the critically intellectual. Jesus was forceful without harshness. He was convivial but never weak. He was austere and not disagreeable. He was critically intellectual while still a young man. I take the accounts in the four Gospels with every critical allowance. He drove out the money-changers and faced death with unmoved courage, yet little children clung to him with joy. He attended the banquets of the rich, but his companions spoke of him as the holy child. He fasted long and prayed all night, but he ate and drank like other men, and spoke of the fullness of life. He gave a new law, at least more positive and profound than those of old time, and was crucified at about thirty. He has all the virtues of the character types and none of their defects. He combines their qualities of excellence in one harmonious whole. I do not accept Klausner's estimate that he was the product of his time and circumstances. He is more. He is a portent in the creative process."

There was a pause while the professor very neatly captured one of my castles.

"You might even say then," I advanced, "that he was a new species in the course of evolution?"

"Exactly," replied he. "That is how I regard him. Moreover, there is a mystery in the consciousness he had of the divine. I do not presume to fathom this, but whenever I read the Good Book, it grips me. He spake as never man spake."

"You do not feel then," I asked, "that the discoveries of Darwin have destroyed the possibility of religious belief?"

"That will depend a little," he answered, "upon what you mean by religion. If you mean

231

the crude anthropomorphism of the early chapters of Genesis and the tribal deity of primitive Judaism, I certainly do. But if by religion you mean that there is an intelligent first cause and that it is possible that man can have a relationship to that first cause—call it God if you prefer—then I do not see how Darwin in any way affects the matter. In one manner of looking at it science and religion have nothing to do with each other. Science investigates the how of things, while religion is the philosophy of the why of things. But in another and deeper way of regarding the matter religion and science are in reality one and the same thing. There can be but one source of all truth in the ultimate. The scientific man may not consider himself religious. He may never go to church. He may reject all creeds. But what he knows he derives from the source of all truth. And in so far as he is successful in the application of his knowledge, he conforms himself to the ultimate laws of being which are, I take it, the laws of God.

232

Now, technically speaking, we use the term religion when we speak of moral or spiritual laws. But this is a narrow use. Moral and spiritual laws come from exactly the same source as those which we call scientific. Darwin himself did not realize the unity of truth. He had the Victorian view of religion. I think that the best type of scientists and the better sort of theologians have gone beyond that narrow conception. They tend to make a synthesis."

"You implied just now," I said, "that you regarded Jesus as an instance of the creation of a new species in the course of the evolutionary process. And I inferred that you so considered him because of his remarkably balanced and universal character and because of his extraordinary insight. But I had supposed that the process of evolution implied, not a mere single instance of a new type, but a continuation and development of that type in other instances."

"Why, just so," he replied. "Have I not said that he started a new course of history? Human

233

beings have in many instances been changed since his time. The process may be slow. But what are two thousand years in the evolutionary ages? The Jurassic age was much longer in working out its results. And there have already been many cases of men and women who have risen very close to his type, if not quite equaled it. There have been, and there may be again, reversions, depressions, in the process, but in the long run the world grows better."

"And that reminds me," he added, running his king's bishop five diagonal squares in the direction of my queen, "that those who minimize the real humanity of Jesus and picture his birth, life, and death as merely something to be looked at as one might look at the Passion Play at Oberammergau or a religious motion picture, a dramatic spectacle to be believed in, do mankind no service. If he were in any sense different from what we are, except in the degree of his perfection of character and the depth of his spiritual insight, he would be valueless to mankind. There must be the possibility of our attaining to his stature. And remember that character is to be judged by what it aims to attain rather than by what it is at the moment."

"Do you mean that we can become what he was?" I asked.

"That is just what I mean," said he.

"Then perhaps you spoke rather too, let us say, scientifically, when, at the beginning of our talk, you minimized the value of the observance of one day in the year as a commemoration of his birth?" I suggested.

"Perhaps I did," he replied.

"Checkmate in three moves," I announced.

"Your game. But at least we are not yet in the twelve-mile limit."

"It is an ancient custom of the day," I admitted.

Next morning the sea, the blue mirror of eternity, gleamed with the dazzling light of the new day.

"Merry Christmas to you, mate," said I—for the captain was on deck.

"Merry Christmas to you, sir," replied the mate.

"And which chapter in the Good Book did you read last night, mate?" I asked.

"I read, sir," said he, "that one where the angels sang at the birth of Jesus." A light came in his face as he added, "And well they might, sir; well they might."

THE BLUE MIRROR [1]

MULTIMILLIONAIRES eat lobster thermidor served on gold plates. There is a tinkle of ice. Obsequious butlers pour cocktails from silver shakers. The aroma of Bacardi fills the air. Delicate vintages from the sunny hills of France mantle the vitreous splendors of Venice.

Pre-war stuff?

Landed last night from the rakish French schooner. You can still see the wicked slant of her masts on the blue line of the horizon. Hull down. Making off on the starboard tack beyond the twelve-mile limit.

A very profitable voyage, monsieur, barring the bribes to the coast-guard.

There has been a winking of lights from the cove. The cases were landed from the long-

[1] "The Blue Mirror" is especially intended for those who understand something of the psychology of meditation.

boat rolling in on the smooth swells in the black night. The bearded sailors in their red berets and tight jerseys handled them with skill. You could see the gleam of brass buttons on the guard's uniform and the bulge of the automatic stuck in his coat pocket as he counted by the light of his electric torch the packet of bills handed over by the honest mate.

"Righto," said the coast-guard.

"Bien, m'sieu'!" said the mate.

Once more the clubs and villas were provided for. "Normalcy" in the mode of living was re-established.

In an age, when the ocean had become a mere waterway, commercialized, commonplace, a canal for barges, tugs, tramp steamers, a farming land for lobster pots, a region of fish ponds and oyster dredges, the Volstead Act suddenly gave us back the era of romance. All that was ever done in the age of the buccaneers, the Spanish Main, the smugglers of French brandy to the shores of Devon, the lurid days of Captain Kidd and Captain Blood, plenty of adventure, derring-do, signals in the dark, swift and perilous voyages, tricking the dull and sleepy government officials, vast organizations of corruption with agents in every department of state, sleek and respectable bankers sitting at high desks and toiling ostensibly over honest ledgers, gunmen, hijackers, shots and murder in the night, corpses of unknown men with olive skins, very well dressed, their rolls of bills intact, their wrist-watches still ticking, with crosses cut on their faces, mysteriously slain, all this and more has been restored to an age that threatened to become prosaic. The sea has reasserted itself.

Let uplifters shriek from platforms and pulpits. Let the long white faces of puritanical preachers drop their jaws. Let the government officials spend the taxes in buying more four-funneled rum-chasers and aeroplanes. The ocean—vast, mysterious, shrouded—still rolls on its romantic way. Poets and historians will transmit the flavors of this picturesque period to posterity. Some great literary artist will arise to write "The Rum-Runner's Revenge; or, Beautiful Bertha, the Bootlegger's Bride."

Little wonder that shore-front property in the "developments" along the New Jersey and Long Island coasts has risen in value to fabulous heights. In the vacation period the tired denizens of crowded cities, thirsting for the taste of adventure, swarm in thousands to the beaches. The uncertainties of vast distances, the unspoiled air, the color and dash of the sea, the imagination of what lies over the horizon, the unknown destinations of strange craft in the offing allure them. The dull world of offices and desks, of counters and dry goods, of clanging trolleys and honking motor cars, of routine and wages, gives way to the primitive yellow sands of the beach, the eternal blue of the great deep, to the human form reduced almost to the ultimate nakedness of prehistoric savagery, and men seek to divest themselves of the shackles of civilization and to return for a day to the primeval youth of the world. The very popularity of the experience threatens to destroy its possibility.

"Southampton," said the Jewish realtor, "Southampton has been very egglesclusive. Ve vill make id cosmobolitan."

You shall see crowds of editors and preachers, bank clerks and shop-girls, college professors and harlots, gangsters and Methodist deacons, school-teachers and gamblers, lawyers and pick-pockets, actors and authors, tired business men and chorus girls, college students and babies, milling along the board walks. For fifty miles east of Brooklyn and all the way from the Highlands down to Barnegat a few feet from where, as Swinburne puts it, "the wind's feet shine along the sea," it is all one city street. At night the electric lights dim the very stars and destroy the moon. The smell of gasoline poisons the salt air. There is a concrete road along the ocean front. Apartment houses overlook the waves. The noise of the surf is drowned by the raucous clamor of hurdy-gurdies and orchestras playing

241

jazz. And just beyond the breakers small boats with advertisements printed on their sails ply to and fro. The very sea is becoming vulgarized.

So one must go beyond the metropolitan area to some more secluded shore to hear any longer the voice of the great deep and to look into the blue mirror of eternity.

II

The Doctor is holding a meditation in the studio on Fifty-seventh Street. The room is lofty and cool. The light is dim but sufficient. There are perhaps thirty people seated on comfortable chairs in a semicircle before the Doctor. On the wall behind the Doctor's chair is a large oil painting. It represents the sea. The sea in a golden light. On the waves the diminutive figure of a man is seen walking. Behind him looms the vague and enormous outline of a much greater man formed from the golden clouds, over-shadowing, guiding. On either side of the paint-

242

ing are charts containing definitions of the
strange terminology the Doctor uses in his medi-
tations. The Doctor is very old. His voice cracks.
But he is alert and keen. The group before him,
mostly women, is intelligent, refined, well-to-do.
I recognize a dramatic author of note and his
wife. The method of meditation employed by
the Doctor helps the dramatic author to get ideas
for his plays. A woman of fashion sits near them,
very rich. Very rich, but unhappy. She is seek-
ing a solution of her problem. An enormous fat
woman sits close by. She hopes to reduce by
the power of "thought waves" without the
trouble of retrenchment at the table. All of the
listeners want something. It is the Doctor's business to cure their needs.

The meditation proceeds slowly. There are
pauses between the sentences. At intervals of
about ten minutes complete silence is maintained
for several minutes. The Doctor supplies the
ideas as one might hold up a piece of illuminated glass for people to look at against the light.

The periods of silence are to be used by the listeners to allow the ideas to sink in. This is a meditation.

One does not always use the periods of silence to consider the thoughts suggested. The mind untrained to the method wanders. The fat woman creaks uneasily in her chair. She may be thinking of food. The playwright's eye rolls upward. He may be working on the last act. The painting of the sea behind the Doctor's chair suggests many things. One dreams of many places, many things.

III

The tall windows of the drawing-room give on a garden. It is a garden in the English manner. Perhaps rather in the New England manner. For each nation has its own type of garden. The meticulous, mathematical elegancies of France. The classical somnolencies of Italy. Why should America import even the irregular and sheltered

Elizabethan richness of our insular ancestors, their peach-trees trained like vines to cling to walls? An American garden then, long and narrow. Its rows of hollyhocks, of snapdragons, of lady-slippers, of poppies, roses, asters and dahlias in their turn, tall flowers and short shrubs, not too carefully trimmed. No dour intransigent Scotch gardener trims this one.

Beyond the garden the lawns spread out, kept vivid in the mists and fogs and moist sea air, mowed to the thick quality of velvet and bordered by darker hedges of box.

From the windows you can see, across the lawns, the dunes and the yellow sands of the beach, the sparse beach grasses bending in the wind. And over and between the dunes the sea. Deep metallic blue. Hard. Solid. The diaphanous sky is tender in comparison. The horizon makes a clear line against the light. It is sharp, defined.

The sea is the reason for the lawns, the garden, the house itself. They are there because the sea is there. They are but frames for the picture.

A setting for the jewel. The green of the lawns together with the touches of gay color in the garden and the yellow sands emphasize and deepen the blue mystery of the ocean, cut by the white edges of the waves and the surf, like the rich color of a mediæval church vestment wrought on hand-looms by religious fingers, silk brocade of indescribable design. Blue is the color of the Virgin, of the sky, of heaven itself. Green, set off with borderings of red, of gold, of pink, is the color of the land. And without the peace and beauty of the garden the sea would lose something of its intensity, its contrast, and its charm. The house and the garden speak of security, stability, human culture. The sea is untamable and vast. Man measures and designs the garden. The sea belongs to God. "His way is in the sea and his paths in the great waters."

Awe and wonder at the sea are in the blood of the race. They go back to the most primitive period of human history. Man is so little, so impotent, so ignorant. The sea is so enormous, so variable, so terrifying. They that went down to the sea in ships saw the wonders of the Lord, the stormy winds arising, the waves as high as heaven, and their hearts failed them for fear. What was beyond the sea? The ancient geographers had no guess beyond the edge of the world and they pictured dreadful dragons guarding the approaches to the eternal voids of space. If you sailed far enough, you would doubtless fall over into the abyss. The sea was surrounded by the mystery of the unknown and unknowable.

"Awe and wonder formed the primitive religions of mankind." The Doctor was speaking. "They are still at the basis of religion. For though we have pushed back the frontiers of knowledge, we have but increased the mystery. The unknown and the unknowable are still with us. We have made the world round and charted the seven seas of the planet on which we live, but in the illimitable blue above sail the multitude of stars and we have penetrated but a short distance into the limits of the universe."

247

And the sea does as well for the average man as any other of the great aspects of nature to stand for the universal and the eternal, for man's ignorance and impotence in relation to the great forces and for his dependence upon conditions which he cannot control. There may be an illusion, but the illusion reflects the reality, as the wide waters of the deep reflect the sky.

I walk through the tall windows of the drawing-room. I pass into the garden and cross the lawns. Down on the beach the great rollers comb and crash with a hollow regular beat. It is early morning and the sun is but an hour or so in the sky. Out over the ocean the clouds are dappled gray and the rays of the sun stream down through the breaks in bars of gold. The sea is a shimmering fluid floor, vast, illimitable, stretching out to the end of all space. The sun is a ball of fire just in the right proportion to give the necessary illumination, nothing more. Your eye is adjusted to the picture. Your imagination responds kindling the elementary emotions. Your feelings are the same as those of some primitive savage who stood on this exact spot fifty thousand years ago and watched the rising sun. The earth is a flat disc, the center of the universe, the sun its lantern, the sky a canopy of light to cover it. The eye of man, his own size, the relative distance of the sun from the earth, the relation of man's size and eye to the curve of the globe, all conspire to deceive him, to build an illusion.

You may have learned from books that the earth is a globe depressed at the poles, but standing there on the beach, it is difficult to believe it. To the eye the earth is flat and the level water proves it. We may have been taught that the sun is so much larger than this planet that, if our earth was thrown into one of the smaller sun spots, it would be in relation but the size of an orange tossed into a cyclone. But such teaching is contrary to the teaching of our senses. And moreover we may have had the assurance of learned professors that the whole ocean in comparison to the sun is but as a drop of water which would sizzle into steam, dry up and disappear, if we came, say, but a few million miles nearer to the orb of day. But this is difficult to imagine. The geocentric conception of the universe is so drilled into the racial consciousness, it so accords with our actual experience, it is so much all we know and all we can understand, that the instruments of education themselves are powerless to eradicate the impression. Yet we do know and admit that the whole planet is so small relatively in the interstellar spaces that from the nearest fixed star it would be utterly invisible even through the strongest telescope. With thought and imagination the sea shrinks to a drop of water and man becomes a veritable nothing in relation to space.

To the mind of the primitive savage such ideas never entered. We have only recently emerged from a mental attitude which still maintained the geocentric theory of the universe. Our practice, our imagination, our emotions

250

and our religion are still colored by the vague illusions that the sea at sunrise conjures up. In this blue mirror we behold the reflection of the universal and the eternal.

IV

And in the garden by the sea a single dew-drop rests on the pink petal of an open rose. More perfect than a pearl of price. A globule of water. In its way it is quite as wonderful and mysterious as the sea itself. It reflects the whole glory of the day. The sun glistens in it. The blue of the sky is there. In the night it had doubtless given back the stars their light or to the moon its flooding glory. A little world. A microcosm. Much in little. Within its limited space perhaps were swift darting animalculæ, microscopic vitalities, as eager for life as the men and women of the milling crowds on the board walks along the beaches at Asbury Park or Atlantic City.

Moreover this globule of hydrogen and oxygen is very old. It seems new and bright as

251

though it had been just created, but in reality it is as old as the world itself, more ancient than the sea. Yesterday perhaps it flowed in the waves offshore or sailed above the land in a cloud. But it has been everywhere. In glacial epochs in the form of ice it moved south to be released by the warmth of the tropic suns, one of a great army that gouged out deep ravines and carved mountains, leaving grooves on the solid rocks. It whirled in ceaseless storms during the geologic ages. It rested as a snowflake upon the highest Andes or drifted on the steppes of Asia. As steam it rose from volcanic depths and floated in mists to fall again into the sea. There it swept the keels of Roman triremes or was dashed along by the oars of Carthaginian galleys. It roared over the deck of the wrecked Hesperus and fell in a gentle shower upon the streets of foreign cities. In an hour it will be gone. You shall look for its place and find nothing but a slight moisture. It has disappeared. But it is not annihilated. The sun has taken it away.

252

But look upward and you will see it drifting off in the mist to moisten a distant field of grain. It has work to do. It is ever busy and has ever been busy. Eternal as the sea. Essential to the universe.

"The primitive savage," the Doctor was saying, "conceived of the earth as the center of the universe. Indeed, we have only recently emerged from the mental attitude that maintained the geocentric theory of the universe. Our practice, our emotions, and our religion are still colored by the vague illusion that the sea at sunrise conjures up. Our language is confined to spatial terms that are based upon this theory. At present we only see the baffling reflections in a mirror."

But in this blue mirror do we not behold the suggestion of the universal and the eternal?

V

In the studio there was silence. And how relative even silence is! The Doctor sat slightly

253

swaying, rhythmically moving his head. The group about him swayed in unison. Some seemed to be asleep. The fat lady nodded over her double chins. Outside, above the deep roar of the great city came the clang of metal, cries of newsboys, honks of motor horns. But there was nevertheless silence in the studio. A relative silence. Very real.

VI

"Now in the speculative contemplation," continued the Doctor, "there is something more in value than a mere poetic and imaginative pleasure. Something beyond mystical appreciation even. Something practical. For the human mind is also a mirror. It not only reflects through the record of the eye and other senses the colors and forms of the universal environment, but it can visualize through the imagination a whole world of events, conditions, circumstances, dreams and visions that may or may not have

254

any parallel in reality. Moreover, the mind is so constituted that it is able to direct in some measure at least the particular objects that it will entertain and reflect.

"The majority of people living on the plane of material experiences reflect in the mirror of their minds the ideas, theories, hopes, and fears of the race inheritance. Responding to actual sense impressions, they translate through the power of their imaginations in a language which they understand such ideas as they and their ancestors have always been accustomed to receive. Hence, upon the surface of their minds, appear the shadows of suspicion, anxiety, terror, anger, envy, lust, the vague dragons that ignorance conjures up on the frontiers of knowledge. They are dominated by prescriptive authority and yield easily to the opinions of the mob. Their reflections are superficial and sordid, like the reflections of a pond or a puddle. Turgid and dull.

"But mirrored in the mind of the student,

255

the scholar, the inventor, the discoverer, the statesman, the scientist, the artist, the musician, the poet, and the mystic are far deeper and lovelier visions. Such men respond with equal or greater velocity to sensation and translate by the creative faculty of the imagination, trained, disciplined or illuminated, into ideas of splendor and of power. For it must be remembered that, like the dewdrop and the globules of water that compose the sea, the elements of man's nature also go back to the beginning of creation and man is stamped with the original genius of the Source of all being. The wisdom and the power of the primeval energy that first moved on substance for the fashioning of forms is itself vibrant in the human mind and rises there to conscious coöperation. The whole is within the part. Man may see in his own interior nature the reflection of the divine. Look deep enough and the creative ideas appear. There is nothing new in the principles which are discovered as new-found laws, nothing actually original in

256

the inventions and combinations that mark the progress of the race. They are merely seen for the first time in the mind where they have in reality existed from eternity. The artist and the scientist turn within to think, as they would say. In reality they are but looking into the mirror of the mind which reflects eternal truth.

"There is something of will in this, something of the power of choice. We can in some measure—the exact measure is quite uncertain—make choice of the images we shall regard or allow to fashion on the mirror of the mind. But we can do little or nothing about the results or consequences of entertaining them. Every image, every idea, every thought, has both an intellectual and an emotional content. The intellectual record is registered on the tissues of the brain in the cells of the gray matter of the cerebrum, much as the needle of a phonograph records the words of a speaker or the notes of a singer. But the emotional content is passed on through the medulla oblongata, down the

257

spinal cord, into the nerves where it is recorded in the ganglia and nervous system. There it may affect the beating of the heart, the respiration of the lungs, the secretions of the glands and the quality of the blood. The depressing and even toxic effects of images which produce fear, anxiety, anger, and regret are well known. And, on the other hand, conceptions that suggest confidence, hope, courage, serenity, joy, freedom, gaiety, and contentment are of the essence of health and well-being. Sunk deep in the emotional nature the content of the images of the mind becomes a part of our habit of thought and our character. It determines the direction of our lives.

"The value to the race of the religious images which have been reflected upon the minds of men for generations cannot be estimated. However crude, imperfect, and even false they may have been in many respects, they answered a purpose in their effect upon character and conduct, in the emergence from savagery and the advance of civilization. When the mediæval mind reflected a sky filled with angels and saints and God seated on an anthropomorphological throne, it had at least a restraining influence. The imagination was filled with gorgeous colors. There were corresponding results—monasticism and chivalry, crusades and cathedrals, the 'Summa' of St. Thomas and the 'Commedia' of Dante. The sixteenth-century Protestant mind reflected a more somber sky, a Miltonic heaven, the stern features of righteousness and judgment, the face of the great Law-giver, none the less potent in its influence upon mankind. And the faint shadows of these past images still tinge the imaginations of multitudes, exercising restraint and impelling to action.

"The revolution in religious thought that is taking place at the present time is due to this same reflective power of the human mind. For what cannot be imagined cannot be believed in. Like the farmer who saw the picture of the giraffe, and declared "There ain't no such animile."

Experience and knowledge determine the nature of the pictures we can form in the mind. The dreams of childhood fade into the light of common day. The college student no longer visualizes the universe in the way of the pictures presented in the Bible. Geographic heavens and literal hells vanish in the light of modern knowledge. The educated person no longer imagines God as an aged patriarch in some remote place. Scriptural and theological pictures do not register.

"There are curious laws about this mirror of the mind, laws as mysterious and unfathomed as those which govern the flow of the tides and ocean currents. For instance, ideas received through the other senses or through the written or spoken word must be translated into terms of sight before they can be fully grasped and realized. Things must be seen, pictured in the imagination centers of the brain, to be understood. McDougall tells us that if these imagination centers are disturbed by some emotion,

260

such as anger or fear, we cannot see well with the eye, no matter how well the optic nerve may function. The eye, curiously, is but an exposed portion of the brain. Our feelings affect its power of vision more than we realize. We see better when we are happy than when we are sad —our emotions affect our thought and determine our judgment. A good feeling is far more important in many instances than a correct conviction; or, rather, it is impossible to have a correct conviction unless the emotions are of a certain kind.

"The things that we can reflect, then, upon the mirror of the mind depend upon the emotions and the emotions in turn are affected by the things reflected. Thus meditation becomes the art of the mystic and a necessity for religious understanding.

"And it is well to remember that it is not alone the things mirrored from without, the new sense impressions, that appear on the surface of the human consciousness of the individual, that

261

must be considered. For like the dewdrop and the waters of the sea, the human mind traces back to the original substance of the universe. It is the heir to the eternal. It contains all things within itself. 'As is the whole, so is the part.' That primal germ or impulse that seized with emotional instinctive wisdom upon the substance out of which the worlds were made and wrought in the chemical elements through an infinite variety of forms, up from inchoate slime, through the primates, the anthropoids, the cave-dwellers, the slowly evolving races, contained within itself all that has since developed. The light of civilization, science, art, the very structure of the brain and the glittering refulgence of thought, all were packed into the original germinal urge. This wisdom was emotional rather than consciously rational. It was instinctive rather than formally mental. But it was the wisdom that made the worlds and that formed the mind of man. Like the kingdom of God, it is within us. Each individual of the race contains the reflection of the whole. Beneath each consciousness the totality of the divine universal knowledge rests. And it is the discovery of this fact that makes us the sons of God. The whole of eternal wisdom gleams in each human mind reflecting omnipotent splendor. If we shall gaze into that mirror, we shall know the truth and the truth shall make us free.

"Imagination, then, is the creative faculty. By virtue of its possession we are said to be made in the image of God."

VII

But let us return to the ever fascinating sea.

In the swift current of the Sound we stop the engine of the yacht's launch and drop the anchor. The small boat dances on the waves up and down with a gyrating motion. Our bodies sway and circle to keep the equilibrium with the hips for a pivot. Round and round like a top. (Excellent exercise for the obese lady in the studio!) Overboard to the windward go the long lines heavily weighted with their lead sinkers, the hooks baited with pieces of mackerel. There is a twitch, a pull. The fish is drawn up wriggling, twisting, squirming, flapping, its eyes dilating, its mouth open and tortured by the cruel hook. It must soon die. Its life and vivid glitter lapse to dull stiffness. The ocean teems with life, life which lasts for its day and then is yielded up to sustain other forms of life. Alas! life lives on life.

At the lower end of the island there is a cliff. Thirty years ago it was an enormous cliff. Enormous and very peculiar. It had been driven upward from the bottom of the ocean in some long past geologic age, huge strata of clay, clay of a great variety of colors. The red, indigo, green, yellow, blue clay in great twisted bands made a contrast to the brown hills and the gray waters, known to mariners far and near. Famous scientists, geologists of note, came long distances to study this strange cliff and wrote learned treatises about it. But now most of it has gone. It has been so worn away by the winter storms that only a fragment of its former glory remains. The tides and currents have carried away what was once a notable landmark.

Change and decay, life and death, the fluid ocean and its moving shores, remind us that nothing is permanent, nothing secure. Heraclitus discovered long centuries ago this eternal flux.

And even as my companion and I discussed the problem, a mutation took place in the very scene. The dark rack of storm gathered to the north. A black line suddenly appeared on the surface of the waters moving rapidly towards us, whipping the waves as it came into white and menacing crests.

"We must run for it," said he, hauling up the anchor.

"I have noticed," said I as the motor began to chug and the launch leaped away, "that the more experience a man has at sea, the more careful he becomes."

"And with reason," answered my compan-

265

ion. "The sea is terrific. It is sudden, pitiless, and cruel. On a fair day it seems to beckon like a wanton, but within an hour it may change to the fury of a blinded and insane giant that strikes without respect of persons and with appalling force. I sometimes watch these summer youths, these harbor mariners, with amazement. In their light craft they toy with death. Only last month, just about here where the rip runs eight miles an hour at the tide, two boys in a small sloop were caught in a squall. Their father and I were up there by the lighthouse utterly powerless to help, watching them through the glass. The wind ripped their light gear to shreds. Their anchor was no better than a child's tin plaything. They were swept out to sea in a smother of foam, their craft rolling bottom upwards. I shall not easily forget the look on their father's face when he dropped the glasses and staggered backward, his hands clutching his head."

266

Perhaps it was this inherent terror of the sea that made St. John in his island vision of the hereafter declare, "There was no more sea."

But later that day I walked again in the garden. The storm had passed. The air was still. The sun poured a flood of light upon the scene. Across the lawns and beyond the dunes lay the sea. Blue. Metallic. Vast. At peace. The rack of the storm had been swept away and the clouds that now appeared were drifting like great ships lazily away to the far horizon. I recalled Rossetti's sonnet,

"Where the cloud-foaming firmamental blue
Rests on the blue line of a foamless sea."

I thought of the security of love, of that fourth dimensional quality which is beyond time and space, of the One Whose habitation is eternity, unmoved by the ebb and flow of tides, the waves of this troublesome world, the flotsam and jetsam along the shores of life, the howling of tempests

267

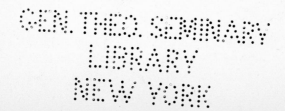

or the blowing winds of chance. I looked for the dewdrop on the petal of the rose. It had vanished. But the sea stood firm. Its voice spoke of the mystery of life. Its blue mirror reflected eternity.

THE END

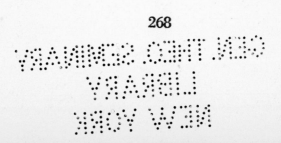